The *da Vinci* Zone

Transcending Perceived Limitations

Robin Byrne

"When you achieve an outcome that is so phenomenal, it redefines what is possible."

Contents

The *da Vinci* Zone

Transcending Perceived Limitations

FOREWORD

My first encounter with Robin Byrne was during a rehearsal for "Jesus Christ Superstar" at the Sioux Empire Community Theatre, located in the historic Orpheum Theatre in downtown Sioux Falls, South Dakota. Robin had been cast as King Herod, while I played Pontius Pilate. My daughter had strongly persuaded me to audition for the role, and my passion for music and this musical eventually led me to succumb to her encouragement. This decision not only allowed me to be part of a memorable theatrical experience but also to forge a meaningful friendship with Robin Byrne. Together, over the next four years, we successfully rebranded the community theatre as The Premiere Playhouse, saving it from financial ruin. Our shared passion for providing artistic opportunities to the community and enhancing the city's cultural landscape was a driving force behind our collaboration. Robin is a distinguished businessman, known for creating the internationally acclaimed Measurable Management Program, a notable vehicle for business and leadership development. During our boating trips on Lake Madison, SD, Robin and I would engage in conversations about his work, as well as my experiences working with President Clinton and Senator Tom Daschle. It was on one of these trips that Robin mentioned an unwritten book, "The da Vinci Zone," sparking my interest. Having witnessed Robin's directorial prowess in another theatrical production, "The Man Who Shot Liberty Valance," I had no doubt about his creative depth. He described "The da Vinci Zone" as a place one reaches when achieving an outcome so phenomenal that it redefines what is possible. In our discussions, Robin referenced Winston Churchill's remarkable achievement of rescuing 350,000 soldiers from the beaches of Dunkirk, despite his advisors' estimates of 50,000. This resonated with me, as I have long admired Churchill as both a politician and an inspirational leader. Years later, over coffee at a local coffee shop, Robin reminded me of our boat conversation and asked if I would write the foreword for his book. I agreed without hesitation. During my tenure as Regional Head of FEMA (Federal Emergency Management Agency), I witnessed countless individuals in dire need of extraordinary assistance. People who, in the blink of an eye, lost everything—homes, possessions, and loved ones. I saw first responders and relief workers, inspired by humanity and compassion, going above and beyond for their fellow man. While they may not have explicitly reached "The da Vinci Zone," their actions certainly embodied its essence, performing beyond all expectations. Such inspiration and determination are contagious. As Robin explains in the following pages, we all have the potential to transcend our perceived limitations, often with astonishing results. In striving to do so, we inspire others to reach for their own "da Vinci Zone."

Richard Paul Weiland

Businessman, Retired Chief Executive Officer of the International Code Council, appointed by President Bill Clinton to the Federal Emergency Management Agency, and Senior Advisor to former U.S. Senator Tom Daschle

A Few Words from the Author

My life today is a far cry from the humble roots that were my accident of birth. Just like everyone, my journey has had many joyous as well as many tragic experiences that shape the person, establish their values and influence the behaviors that define how others perceive you.

I was born in the bedroom of a tiny house in a small village in County Durham, Northeast England, called Witton Park. At the time of my birth, Witton Park was officially listed as the poorest village in England, with 90% unemployment and was scheduled by the government for demolition. We had no electricity, no hot water except for the kettle and no flushing indoor toilet. The outside toilet was emptied with a shovel by two men from the local council whose job it was to empty all of the toilets in the village armed with those two shovels and a tin bathtub. My dad was one of those two men. Rather than be one of the 90%, he was prepared to shovel shit to put food on the table.

He was James McWilliam Byrne (Jimmy) and my mother Margaret (Peggy to everyone) inspired me and my two older brothers to work hard for what you want and to do whatever it takes to rise above. When my dad died aged 93, he was not wealthy, but he did own his house and he had more income than he needed to live on. My true inheritance, however, and the inheritance of my two older brothers, was one of strong moral character. Stand up to the bullies but never become the bully.

I have been to Nelson Mandela's house in Soweto, South Africa and poked my fingers into the bullet holes in the brickwork. This was a man who knew how to fight but more importantly, he knew how to forgive. This was a man who ignored the perceived limitations of his birthright to reach beyond what others thought possible. He wrote a personalized message in a copy of his autobiography that he gave to my good friend Andy Andrews, who then owned the Graduate Institute of Management and Technology in Johannesburg. The handwritten words inside the book cover said:

"Thank you for all that you have done for the South African Economy."

Nelson Mandela.

Andy showed this to me and said, "That's your Measurable Management Program that he's talking about. He's thanking you too."

Today I am a US citizen living in Sioux Falls, South

Dakota, one of the USA's hidden secrets. Governor Bill Janklow, before he passed away, used to have my boys over to his house regularly as they were best friends with his grandchildren. My good friend Rick Weiland, who wrote the foreword to this book, ran against John Thune for the US Senate after he had previously served Bill Clinton and Senator Tom Daschle. I love to hear his memories of being in the Oval Office, of having dinner sitting next to Barabara Streisand at a fundraiser and of him sitting in Gregory Peck's study holding the Oscar for *To Kill a Mockingbird.*

When I was sworn in as a US citizen at the Washington Pavilion on Dec 7th, 2018, Senator John Thune was the very first person to shake my hand and congratulate me on my citizenship. As the Republican Conference Chair, he holds the third-ranking position in the US Senate.

The first thing that I did on exiting the doors of the auditorium that staged the ceremony was to walk over to a table that had been set up in the lobby and register to vote.

A United Nations Positive Peace Award nomination and some business success as the author of the Measurable Management Program have put a vast distance, both geographically and metaphorically, between my life today and the early austerity that was my birthright. It is amazing what we are all capable of when, like Mandela, we set our sights on something that may seem unattainable and reach for it. I refer to it as reaching for The da Vinci Zone. It is the place that you arrive at when you achieve an outcome that is so phenomenal, it redefines what is possible. I am no Mandela, not even close. I have not yet touched The da Vinci Zone and perhaps I never will, but in reaching for it, I have managed to rise higher than anyone might expect the son of a shit shoveler to rise.

I sat down to author a book that I know from experience will be helpful to all businesses regardless of size, location, market sector, for profit or not for profit and to make it entertaining. If you are the owner of a one-man business, I know that you will find this book just as meaningful and helpful to you as will the CEO of an international corporation. If you genuinely want your company to stand out from others as one that has done phenomenal things for your customers, employees, and your community, then keep reading. If you are looking to align the whole organization behind your vision or if you want to breath fresh life into existing initiatives that are losing momentum, then keep reading. If you simply want your new or your longstanding business to thrive, then keep reading.

The United Nations and the US Air Force have already described the Measurable Management approach to business and leadership development as "*Phenomenal.*" Hundreds of diverse businesses have already used it to reach towards The da Vinci Zone and in so reaching, they have made giant leaps forward.

Keep an open mind as you read this. Indeed, that is exactly where we are going to begin, by looking at the open mind of Leonardo da Vinci and by applying his brand of self-belief to creating positive outcomes—outcomes that transcend perceived limitations, taking you further than you ever thought possible.

Giant Leaps at High Velocity!

The da Vinci Zone is very real. To reach for it is to honestly believe that unreal outcomes are absolutely possible. The evidence is there. Just reach for it.

Robin Byrne

Chapter One

Think Like da Vinci

Leonardo da Vinci is regarded by many to be the most divergently talented individual ever to have lived. Wikipedia justifies this claim by recognizing his accomplishments as a painter, sculptor, architect, musician, scientist, mathematician, engineer, inventor, anatomist, geologist, cartographer, botanist, and writer. They drive the point home by referring to Leonardo as the archetype of the Renaissance man, a man whose unquenchable curiosity was equaled only by his powers of invention and widely considered to be one of the greatest painters of all time. According to American art historian and educator Helen Gardner, the scope and depth of his interests were without precedent, and "his mind and personality seem to us superhuman, the man himself mysterious and remote."

It would be difficult to argue with any of the above apart from the word superhuman. I do not think that Leonardo da Vinci was superhuman. In fact, from a physiological point of view, he was as human as the rest of us. The majority of Daves are born with the potential to be a da Vinci. We all have the same plumbing if you like, but we do not necessarily have as many of our stop valves open as da Vinci had. What I mean by this is that his mind was somehow more open than the minds of what we consider to be "normal people" and this "open all valves condition" flooded his mind with creativity, inventiveness and artistry allowing him to excel in an astonishing number of disciplines. This is the foundation of thinking like da Vinci.

How many other da Vinci's have there been that did not get the recognition that Leonardo benefited from? How many were dismissed as "crazy" or "possessed" and were persecuted for simply being born in the wrong place at the wrong time? Is it possible that one or more may be walking among us today?

Was Leonardo neurodivergent? Neurodiversity is a term used to explain the theory that there is not just one specific way for the brain to work, that there is not just one way of thinking, learning, or behaving. Although the term relates to the diversity of all people's thinking, it is most often associated with those who are positioned somewhere on the autism spectrum. We know of people with varying degrees of autism who, despite these often-extreme symptoms that make socializing with others difficult, seem to be capable of doing amazing things mathematically, musically, artistically and in all the other things that require extraordinary gifts. These gifts and talents are clearly far beyond the level of accomplishment that one would expect of the so-called "normal" or average person. Often referred to as savants such individuals amaze us with their ability to recall data or dates and statistics. Some are gifted musically and can reproduce note for note, chord for chord, the most complex pieces of music after listening to it only once. I am not a medical expert or a neuroscientist so if my terminology should seem clumsy or even offensive, I can only assure you that this is not my intention.

Stephen Wiltshire is autistic and is a world-renowned artist who was featured in 1987 at the age of 12 on a BBC TV documentary entitled "The Foolish Wise Ones." He was seen on camera looking at extraordinarily complex buildings with intricate design details, and after studying the building visually for a minute or two, he was able to draw the building and recreate every detail from memory. These drawings were often done days or weeks after viewing the building, and the accuracy of his drawings astonished the world. In 2001, another BBC documentary entitled "Fragments of Genius" saw Stephen take a 15–20-minute helicopter ride over the City of London. He goes on to create from memory a stunning drawing of London from the air, covering everything in a four mile radius. People who live and work in the enormous variety of buildings featured in his panoramic drawing are amazed to see that he reproduces exactly the minute details of their building, getting the number of floors and windows precisely correct.

Stephen Wiltshire creating his drawing of London from the air. Image from www.inspiremykids.com

We do not know how or why this phenomenon occurs, but savants are gifted across a wide range of disciplines, although individually, they usually display talent in one area. We cannot explain it and the individual cannot tell you how they do what they do, they just can do it! It is as if the stop valve to that specific talent was left open and they were allowed to show genius in that area. Stephen Wiltshire uses his Visual Memory ability to concentrate exclusively on architecture; da Vinci however, seemed to excel in everything that he attempted. Even the recognized genius of Nobel Prize winner Albert Einstein was narrow in comparison to da Vinci. Wikipedia describes Einstein as a theoretical physicist, philosopher, and author. By any standard, this is impressive but compared to Leonardo da Vinci's Wikipedia credits, even Einstein looks almost ordinary.

The famous photo taken by Arthur Sasse in 1951.
Source: Wikipedia
Physicist and Philosopher Prof. Albert Einstein

This higher state that Leonardo da Vinci seemed to operate in, this "all stop valves open" state is something that I am going to refer to as "The da Vinci Zone." While Einstein was definitely in The da Vinci Zone, Leonardo clearly had many more stop valves open than Albert. Leonardo was completely immersed in the Zone while Albert simply paddled up to his knees. Getting into The da Vinci Zone means that the individual or the organization **transcends the perceived limitations** that restrict us and without this restriction, they can reach a level of performance that redefines what we believe is possible. To dismiss this theory out of hand is to immediately submit to your perceived limitations. Just pause for a moment and open up a stop valve to the possibility that this seemingly unreal theory might actually be a sound one.

To accept perceived limitations is not thinking like da Vinci.

Perhaps like Einstein, savants are partially in The da Vinci Zone, having one or more stop valves open to their particular talents. The rest of us are capable of entering The da Vinci Zone from time to time even if we only enter the zone for a fleeting moment. That fleeting moment can often be described as a **Flash of Genius**. Some people however like Einstein seem to have more flashes than others; they enter the zone more frequently and sometimes stay there a little longer than a moment or two. Was John F Kennedy reaching for The da Vinci Zone when he declared in his "Special Message to the Congress on Urgent National Needs," on May 25, 1961, before a joint session of Congress that the United States should set as a goal the "landing of a man on the moon and returning him safely to the earth" by the end of the decade? Kennedy knew that the Soviet Union held the lead in the space race, but he insisted that the USA should strive to take that position from the Soviets because he believed that "in many ways it may hold the key to our future on earth."

Many thought it was impossible, a ridiculous dream but JFK was a visionary, he was thinking like da Vinci. Imagine what people might have thought when da Vinci designed plans for a helicopter, a submarine and a heart valve, hundreds of years before the technology to build these inventions even existed. They may have questioned his sanity. JFK, however, had the advantage of knowing that the technology to get to the moon did exist, but it would take **creativity, inventiveness, artistry,** and much **inspiration** to achieve a successful outcome. **These are the very qualities that Leonardo da Vinci possessed and excelled in.** The rest is history, as American astronaut Commander Neil Armstrong became the first man to set foot on the moon on July 20, 1969. He showed his human fallibility when he made his famous misquote: "One small step for [a] man, one giant leap for mankind." It did not matter that he left out the word [a] because the achievement was truly historic and amazing; the achievement was in the Zone.

When we get into The da Vinci Zone, we can do phenomenal things. Everyone has the potential to touch the Zone or even to get into the Zone and it is right that we should strive to get there even if we never quite make it because simply by attempting to get there, we can raise the quality of our outcomes beyond expectations. They may not always be phenomenal but exceptional positive outcomes are frequently the by-product of reaching for the phenomenal.

Organizations are also very capable of getting into The da Vinci Zone. JFK's thinking was visionary, but he needed all of NASA to work collectively as a team and transcend traditional ideas, rules, patterns, and relationships if his dream was to be fulfilled. He needed everyone on the project to reach for The da Vinci Zone and to be inspired to do the impossible and take that "Giant Leap for Mankind." Imagine how many Giant Leaps for Mankind could be made if more organizations attempted to reach for The da Vinci Zone.

We are taught in Business Schools the world over that our objectives should be realistic, measurable and have a timescale for achievement. I disagree with every one of those Business Schools. **To achieve unreal things, you need to be unrealistic!** Making our objectives realistic is to place limitations on our potential achievements. In reaching for those unrealistic goals, we can still achieve outcomes far greater than those previously thought to be realistically possible. What great discoveries might we unearth as a natural by-product of striving for the unrealistic?

Was Walt Disney being unrealistic when he told his employees that he wanted to turn the swamplands of Florida into a city of the future with transport for everyone by monorail? Some thought it was unrealistic, but Disney was thinking like da Vinci. He said, "**If you can dream it, you can do it.**" Similarly, was the founder of the Virgin Brand, Richard Branson being unrealistic when he decided to build a space port in New Mexico and offer passenger rides into space? It is this kind of dreaming endorsed by Walt Disney that has taken Branson from music shop owner to recording company impresario to airline owner, railway company owner and space travel explorer. It has driven him personally to attempt to set speed records for crossing the Atlantic by powerboat and high altitude around the world ballooning, not always meeting with success but always striving for it. It has taken Branson from **vinyl records to world records** and perhaps to building the first hotel in outer space. It's OK to be unrealistic and perhaps all organizations should have at least one unrealistic objective without a timescale. How does the Board Room know what is "unrealistic"? How do they know what their people are capable of doing, producing, inventing, creating, refining or selling?

Looking to take your organization to the Next Level is simply setting your sights too low. Aim higher, aim much higher, aim for the da Vinci Zone.

Organizations are organic. They are made up of people. Regard these people as the mind of the operation, the brains if you like and to get into the da Vinci Zone, we need to tap into the **creativity, inventiveness,** and **artistry** of each and every one of those workers. We need to open all the stop valves and let the organization start to think a little like da Vinci. We need to take a positive approach to positivity. When we are successful at getting an organization to truly attempt to do positive things for its customers, its employees, and its community, it is impossible to stop positive things happening for the organization. It's a natural by-product of shifting the focus from products, services, and production to the needs of customers, employees, and communities. If a single person can look to the positive and do phenomenal things, so can a group of people. If one organization can do something truly phenomenal, so can other organizations. If reaching for The da Vinci Zone became the aspiration of every organization, then Giant Leaps would happen much more frequently.

This is why Measurable Management® was nominated for the United Nations Positive Peace Award for "*its phenomenal ability to deliver positive outcomes*" It is a positive program that helps organizations to achieve the phenomenal. When "Celebrate Positive," the organizing body for the United Nations Positive Peace Awards, reviewed the Measurable Management® nomination, they approved it because of the sheer volume of positive outcomes that this amazing program has generated for many organizations, their customers, employees, and their communities. I visited a US Air Force base that had recently implemented Measurable Management®. They described it as *without doubt the most effective program for making things happen that we have ever experienced.*"

The organizers of the Southwestern Lean Summit in Tulsa, OK, described it as *"unnervingly simple yet powerfully effective."*

Measurable Management® helps organizations reach for The da Vinci Zone. Organizations can do phenomenal things when they truly engage their employees and inspire them. Measurable Management® provides a vehicle for making things happen, phenomenal things. It helps the organization to open the stop valves and start to think like da Vinci.

Very few organizations have ever been in The da Vinci Zone. To be there is to be truly exceptional. I smile to myself when I hear people in Fortune 500 companies tell me, sometimes with a little touch of arrogance that "we already do that" because I know that it's not true. **I know**

that they believe that they already do that, but the reality is if they were truly in The da Vinci Zone or even reaching for it, they would be doing things so amazingly differently compared to other organizations that it would be impossible for them not to stand out from the crowd. In truth, they are blending in quite nicely with everyone else. You can count on the fingers of one hand the number of companies that genuinely try to "think like da Vinci" and get into the Zone, the rest are deluding themselves. Their self-belief is unquestionable, but then if they didn't honestly believe that "we already do that," they would not be delusional; they would simply be dishonest. Perhaps, like some organizations that have been in the Zone or close to it at some time in their history, they falsely believe that they are still there. They cling to their past glories, wrongly believing that they are still great when, in reality, their empires are in decline. It doesn't have to be that way. **If you can recognize your own reality, you've made the first step towards changing it.**

Many of you will be familiar with the Jim Collins book "Good to Great." I, however, have to admit to having never read it, and it might be good or even great but to me, the title is very off-putting. How many readers of this bestselling book have failed to make it to being Great because, at the outset, they didn't recognize their own reality? Too many companies think that they are good when, in reality, they are mediocre. The problem is that none of us like to admit to mediocrity. We readily admit to the fact that we can always improve we just do not admit to ourselves and others the truth about our current position. The da Vinci Zone is beyond Great. It is so far above Great that many will never realize the goal of touching the Zone. This should never deter anyone from trying, however, because in aspiring to reach the Zone, you will achieve many things that may fall short of da Vinci but will still be way beyond being merely Great. Achievements that will make you question what is possible, that will satisfy you enormously and inspire you and others to do even more amazing things.

Whatever the current position of your organization happens to be, you need to recognize **that the best consultants that any organization can have, already work for it**. The workforce not only knows what is not working in the organization, but often they have innovative ideas, sometimes phenomenal ideas of how to fix it. Organizations just are not as good as they believe themselves or delude themselves to be at opening the stop valves and **engaging the gifted**.

It is essential to put arrogance and egos aside. "We already do that" has no place here. We need to know that we do not know everything. **Knowing that we don't know everything is a good place to be**, it is the logical place to be for us to start opening ourselves up to amazing possibilities. Does your organization engage the gifted? Can you recognize your own reality? Are you standing out from the crowd in a way that is so obvious that its common knowledge to everyone? Are you reaching for The da Vinci Zone? Are you thinking like da Vinci?

Are you sure?

CHAPTER TWO

THE "OH SHIT" SYNDROME

Leonardo da Vinci was clearly a forward-thinking individual, a visionary who looked to the future and imagined what it could be like. His designs for the submarine, helicopter, twin hull and flying machine clearly demonstrate his ability to look ahead and think beyond the limitations of the times in which he lived.

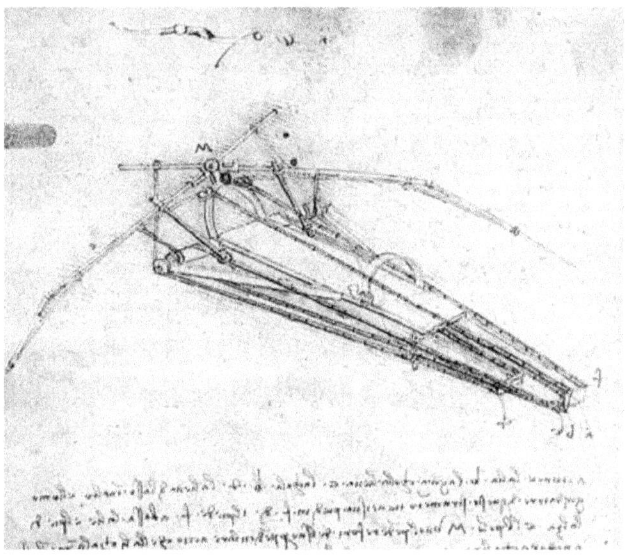

da Vinci's design for a hang glider-like flying machine

It seems so obvious that in order to move forward, you must look ahead, and yet many organizations are moving forwards by walking backward. This quite common scenario is what some others and I refer to as the "Oh Shit" Syndrome. This is my explanation of what it is and why it happens.

Imagine that you have a vacancy for a supervisor position and that you are looking internally to the workforce to find an individual to fill that vacancy. You have a particularly good worker (let us call him Hank) who has worked on the line for over five years and exemplifies everything that a good operator should be. In your opinion, Hank is clearly the best candidate for the supervisor vacancy. He understands the business, his colleagues respect him, and his annual reviews/appraisals have consistently been excellent.

So, on Friday, Hank is at work happily doing the job that he has done for over 5 years and sitting well inside of his comfort zone. On Monday, we yank Hank from the line and surprise him by making him the supervisor, and on Monday morning, he starts his new position. The first thing that goes through Hank's mind is, "Oh shit what do I do?" He has never been a supervisor before and now, instead of being one of the guys, he is now their boss. Hank is now sitting well outside of his comfort zone.

Human nature then kicks in and Hank jumps right

back into his comfort zone by turning around and putting his hands on his old job. He starts telling his people what to do and how to do the job. Time goes by and Hank has eventually become an excellent supervisor either by self-determination or good training, but now he is no longer uncomfortable, in fact the opposite is now the case. Hank has a new comfort zone doing the supervisor job that has been his now for a few years. The one thing we all know about change is that it is going to happen whether you like it or not and soon, there is a middle management vacancy that you know Hank will be perfect for.

So, on Friday Hank is at work happily doing the supervisor job that he has done for several years now, and he is sitting well inside his comfort zone. On Monday we yank Hank from his desk and surprise him with the middle management job. The first thing that goes through Hank's mind is… yes, you have guessed… "Oh shit what do I do? I'm outside of my comfort zone." Once again, human nature kicks in and Hank steps back into his comfort zone, turns around and puts his hands on his old job and starts telling the supervisors how to supervise.

The more frequently this happens, the easier it is to visualize a leadership team steadily walking backward into the future, forever interfering with the job that they used to have instead of thinking like da Vinci and turning around to face the future and delivering their share of the business plan through the people who report into them. This is the "Oh Shit" Syndrome or, as others sometimes describe it, "Managing through the Rear View Mirror."

This situation is sadly quite common. We often promote our best people to positions that we have made little or no effort to prepare them for. We place them into their new role and the "Oh Shit" Syndrome kicks in. If they are lucky, we provide them with some training to help them better cope with their new and uncomfortable surroundings. Some organizations are better than others and attempt to avoid the Syndrome by having processes in place for identifying those with supervisory and leadership potential. They develop these skills with training and development before the individual is placed in their leadership position. This is like my own experience at Xerox, where I went through a very thorough management development program while I was still a salesperson and before I was promoted to Sales Manager. This approach must be much better for everyone than the Oh Shit Syndrome, but is it the best approach?

If you want your organization to think like da Vinci, to transcend your perceived limitations, look ahead and move towards The da Vinci Zone, then you need **everyone** in the organization to think and act like leaders. The typical team member may never become a supervisor, but you may need them to lead a project improvement team if they have had a good improvement idea. How can they do this effectively if you never provide them with the tools and skills to become effective?

I have met only a few CEO's who genuinely want everyone in the organization to act like a leader or a manager. These forward thinkers have recognized that leadership, decision making and problem-solving are not the exclusive domain of managers.

Lee Schull, the CEO of a family-owned business that supplies building products to lumberyards and retail outlets, achieved phenomenal results by deciding that he wanted everyone in the organization to act like a manager. He gave them the authority within financial controls to make improvements without seeking approval. **Importantly he also gave them permission to make mistakes.** He didn't mind if their attempt to improve something didn't always work. It was good that they were trying to make it better and mostly, the outcomes were better.

When Lee took over the business in the early nineties it was producing respectable revenues in the region of $10m per year. Within ten years this had grown to over $100m per year. They buy from manufacturers and sell a complete range of building products and supplies to lumber yards. These are the typical products that any construction company would need to construct a home or commercial building.

I worked with Lee's company implementing Measurable Management in their key locations throughout the Midwest.

In 2008, the subprime collapse created a severely depressed market, with the number of new homes in sharp decline. Numerous manufacturers supplying the company reported drops in the demand for their products by as much as 30 to 50%. In this very same downward cycle, Lee's company achieved record sales and was able to do so without increasing their costs.

Lee had realized that Measurable Management® would give everyone in the organization the tools and the freedom to make good leadership decisions. Like JFK's man on the moon objective, Lee also had Key Issues or Objectives that held the key to their future. By encouraging or even inspiring **everyone** in the organization to look ahead and focus on their core customers, they used that key to unlock potential and transcend their perceived limitations. In doing so, they were able to gain an enormous advantage over their competitors without lowering their prices. By reaching for The da Vinci Zone and involving everyone in the company, they also began to truly engage with their customers in a way that made them significantly stand out from the crowd. When you dare to reach for The da Vinci

Zone you really can transcend your perceived limitations and achieve levels of performance way beyond what was previously thought to be possible. Not every time but some of the time. That is exactly what happened to Building Products Inc. They continued to thrive when the rest took a dive. A survey of customers revealed that they significantly outperformed their competitors in customer service. The speed, frequency and accuracy of deliveries had been the deciding factor in choosing Building Products Inc. as their preferred supplier. One customer was quoted as saying, "They are like my own personal warehouse."

Lee Schull is quick to point out that "through Measurable Management, we had succeeded in developing a workforce that is both customer-focused and financially aware."

Building Product's results are proof of what can be achieved when you engage and empower everyone in the organization to serve the customer. By engaging everyone and making them all leaders, they avoided the Oh Shit Syndrome. They faced everyone forwards and aligned the entire workforce behind their customer service objectives. This enabled them to deliver measurable improvements and successfully change attitudes and culture within the organization. I am not saying that they were in the Zone, or even close to it, but by simply reaching for it, they loosened a few stop valves and transcended their perceived limitations. They achieved levels of performance way beyond those of their competitors in an economy that crippled many others. Their competitors were restricted from doing so because of their conditioned acceptance of their perceived limitations, their lack of engagement and empowerment with employees and customers.

Once again, we must always remember that the best consultants that an organization can have, already work for them. When you can facilitate that expertise into a culture that is both customer-focused and improvement-driven, you can and will impact the bottom line in a way that is "unnervingly simple, yet powerfully effective." If a medium-sized, family-owned business can transcend perceived limitations and do phenomenal things, so can a Fortune Company, a health authority, a charity, a government, or a start-up. Turn yourself and everyone else in the organization around, look ahead, loosen a few stop valves, and have the courage to **make everyone a leader**.

CHAPTER THREE
CORPORATE CONSTIPATION

How else could I follow the "Oh Shit" Syndrome?

Many of us have whined as we dined in the corporate cafeteria of training and development. A veritable banquet of "Lean" cuisine, one delicious training course served up after another, followed by role-play for dessert smothered in acronyms and washed down with a magnum of motivation. The menu changes with every flavor of the month, but the basic ingredients always seem to stay the same and it is never ever cheap. All too frequently we pay consulting companies to provide a gourmet chef only to end up with acid reflux, indigestion, and corporate constipation.

Is it any wonder that having consumed these tasty morsels our people return back to work, and nothing seems to change? They still do the same things the same way that they did before they swallowed the training course. Those who were hungry for development are still hungry, their appetites unsatisfied and their thirst for improvement unquenched. Leadership training is often the course that gives us more indigestion than any other.

Why do we need leaders anyway? What purpose do they serve? To lead is to show the way to others, but Measurable Management contradicts this idea. Managers and supervisors are encouraged to no longer show people what to do and instead, you need to motivate and inspire your people to create an effective solution of their own. This is a good thing because the ownership of the solution ends up sitting right where it should. It rests with those who need to implement it and therefore, the likelihood of resistance to change is extremely low. Motivation, therefore, tends to sit exceedingly high on the list of roles and responsibilities for supervisors, managers, and team leaders and not surprisingly therefore, Leadership and Motivation are often featured as a "Healthy Option Combo" or the "Chef's Special" on many a training and development menu.

Sadly, many leaders are much better at de-motivating than they are at motivating others and in any case, most leaders really do not allocate very much of their time to motivating their people. My views on this are rooted in my belief that most people start out well-motivated and really do want to do an excellent job regardless of where we work or who we work for. Nobody wants to do a bad job. We all want to do well and go out there and score a goal, make a touchdown, or save the day. Nobody ever says to themselves, "Today I want to be average," unless of course they happen to be diabolical to begin with and consider average to be a huge improvement. I therefore feel that we do not always need a course to teach us how to motivate people, we just need to stop de-motivating them. We need as leaders to learn how to recognize de-motivational behavior in ourselves and stop doing it.

Many organizations that are successful probably have a motivated workforce. In other words, they likely have leaders who de-motivate people less frequently than their less successful competitors. We might even place these organizations that mess up less frequently in the "Good to Great" category. They are there because they have managed to maintain a motivated workforce and enjoy the extra momentum that this brings. The big question is, "How do we move up from the Good to Great league towards The da Vinci Zone?" Even organizations with motivated people can find this difficult. They know that they can improve and indeed they strive to do so, but they have their perceived limitations that shape their beliefs of what is possible. These limitations are usually reinforced by everyone in the organization who wants to stay inside their comfort zones. These perceived limitations act like blockages preventing Giant Leaps and significant innovation. The organization is effectively constipated, and the solution for this corporate constipation for many is to take a swift and often ineffective leadership laxative.

Sales and Marketing departments produce the sales

incentive laxative, and we might see an improvement in volume at the expense of margin. Manufacturing Departments look to narrow the upper and lower control limits on their process improvement run charts and possibly rework is reduced. I am not sure that run charts and laxative belong in the same sentence, but my often crude and basic sense of humor will not permit me to leave this out.

What can we do to motivate everyone to truly excel and move us towards The da Vinci Zone? The problem is that we are treating the symptoms with our leadership laxatives when we really need to change the menu and stop thinking of Leadership and Motivation as some kind of antacid relief afterthought.

To transcend perceived limitations, motivation alone is simply not enough. If you want to transcend these "make believe" limitations you need much more, you need Inspiration. The true role of leadership is to inspire others in the much same way that JFK inspired NASA with his "put a man on the moon and return him safely to earth" speech and Winston Churchill inspired a whole British nation with his "We will fight them on the beaches, and we will never surrender" speech. Motivation and Inspiration are not the same things; inspiration touches the heart and the spirit of the individual in a way that also engages their desires.

To truly inspire, you must ignite the desire!

Wow! Do we need a course in speech writing? Obviously not! We clearly need to learn some behaviors that will enable us to engage our people emotionally and inspire them to do phenomenal things. By engaging with people and understanding their emotions and how strongly they feel about something, you can begin to understand the desires that drive them. Desires are much stronger than wants. We will try much harder to obtain something that we desire than we will for something that we simply want or would like to have. We must also believe that our perceived limitations are exactly that, "perceived". Every problem, no matter how impossibly huge it appears to be, has a solution; the challenge lies in finding that solution. Walt Disney was right when he said:

"If you can dream it, you can do it."

You may think that my frame of reference is narrow and that I keep using the same people as examples. The truth is the da Vinci's of this world are extremely rare individuals and that is what makes reaching for The da Vinci Zone so much more appealing than simply continuously improving. Continual Improvement even sounds slow and as it never has a finish line, it can seem a little de-motivational. Getting into The da Vinci Zone is much more exciting, bringing about improvements in quantum leaps and on the rare occasions that you may actually get to experience being there, I imagine it to be enormously satisfying and gloriously inspirational.

If you think that in order to do this, you have to be some kind of Psychologist and that it's going to be way too difficult to understand, then you have just created another perceived limitation and you are in danger of letting this perception defeat you and prevent you from reaching for the Zone.

In my book *Cultural Change through Measurable Management,* I introduce two amazingly simple models that are easy to understand and easy to implement. These two models make it extremely easy for anyone to emotionally engage with others and then to encourage, motivate and occasionally inspire others to do very exceptional things. The outcomes from this emotional engagement to be fair are not always inspirational, but through engaging people and by encouraging them to make an improvement, you are doing a good thing. If you can then motivate them to do something good, then that is also a particularly good thing and the inspirational outcomes, which begin to happen increasingly frequently, are the icing on the cake. This icing tastes much nicer than the artificial temporary sugar fix served up in the training and development cafeteria.

The first of these models is the Thinking, Feeling and Willing Model and I will explain it so as not to tease you like some drawn-out social media video outlining the Secret to Success or some other such quackery.

There are many theories about how people's minds work and what their motives are, but it is accepted that we tend to operate on three levels: the Thinking, Feeling, and Willing levels and that we move between these levels constantly and sometimes very rapidly. It is safe to assume that as you read this you are operating on the Thinking level:

On the **Thinking** level, we absorb information; we process facts. We receive, digest, and communicate information. This information can be received by any of our senses and will trigger a reaction within us. It may be an impulse to act, to respond or it may simply be a feeling.

On the **Feeling** level, we react to people, events, and information. We experience moods and emotions such as happiness, sadness, liking, disliking, anxiety, humor, and anger. These feelings usually trigger our actions. How we feel about something influences how motivated we are to react in either a positive or negative way.

On the **Willing** level, people are motivated (or de-motivated). They commit themselves to an action, they work towards an aim, they make the effort.

Our friend in bed here takes in some information on the **Thinking** level. The alarm clock is telling him it is time to get up. There may be some other information, however that we cannot see… His nose may be telling him how cold the room is, and his feet may be telling him how warm the bed is. On the **Thinking** level, therefore, all this information tells him that it is time to get up, but quite naturally, on the **Feeling** level, he does not feel like he wants to. He lacks the motivation. His reaction on the **Willing** level, therefore, is to lie there a little longer. He is motivated to stay in bed, and he is de-motivated to get up and head for work. Eventually on the **Thinking** level, he receives more information, i.e., the clock is telling him that it is now a few minutes later. On the **Feeling** level, he may become worried about being late for work and getting into trouble. This feeling triggers off his **Willing** level and he becomes motivated to rush and dress to avoid trouble by being late for work.

We can easily understand why he acts as he does

because we have begun to engage with his emotions and therefore, we start to understand how the quality and type of information that we communicate on the **Thinking** level shapes how strongly we **Feel** and influences how **Willing** or motivated we are to act.

If you understand this model and you can see and agree with the logic behind it, then applying it to work situations is much easier than you may at first imagine. This ease and simplicity come courtesy of our second model, the Perceptions Attitudes and Behavior Model.

We exhibit behaviors and depending on what these are, if they are seen by others, then those watching take in our behavior on the Thinking level. If a speaker at a conference appears to trip on the way to the podium and then slurs their opening remarks, those watching may think rightly or wrongly that the speaker is slightly intoxicated. On the Thinking level we are beginning to develop within us a **Perception** of the speaker. This **Perception,** accurate or inaccurate, shapes how we feel about the speaker and on the Feeling level, our **Attitudes,** positive or negative, are beginning to form. Our **Attitude** reflects how strongly we feel and on the Willing level, it influences our **Behavior.** We may decide to get up and leave if we think that the speaker has been drinking. We may get him a chair or a glass of water if we perceive him to be ill and feel that he needs our help. Our **Behavior** is directly influenced by our **Attitudes** or feelings which are in turn shaped by our thoughts and **Perceptions**.

To influence and encourage positive behavior in others, we simply need to look to our own behavior as it is our own behavior that creates the perception in their minds that will influence their behavior towards us. Your behavior begets their behavior and positive behavior begets positive behavior. If you can improve their perception of you or create positive perceptions in the minds of others, then their behavior towards you will be positive also. They have no choice. Now let us make it ridiculously easy to make use of this knowledge. There is one single behavior that you can display that will take you at least 70% of the way towards creating a positive perception of you as a leader in the minds of those that you are trying to lead. By regularly displaying this behavior, you will influence positive outcomes by creating positive perceptions. You will also engage people in a very real and emotional sense. You can work miracles if you just make a conscious effort to LISTEN.

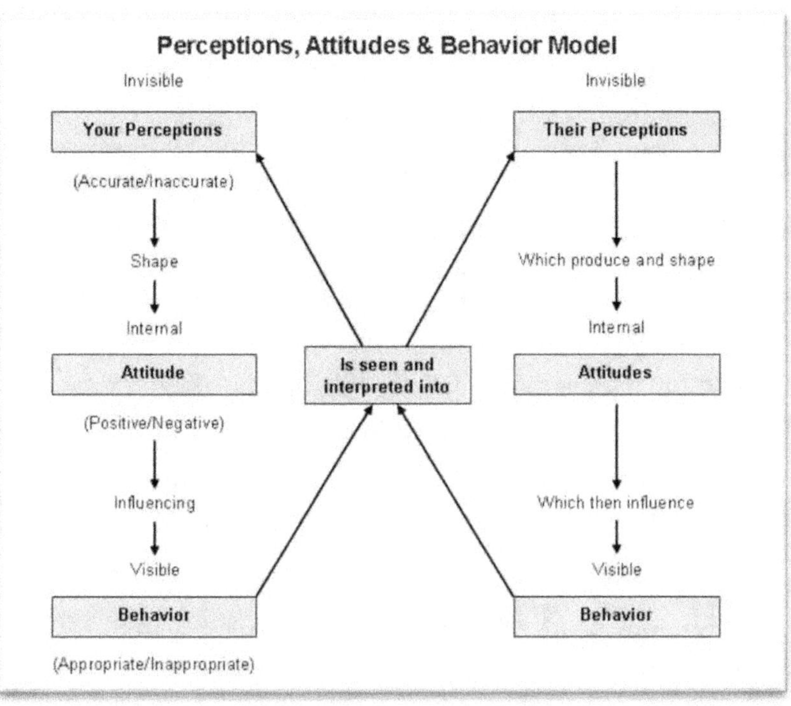

I know that you have heard that before, but there is a dramatic difference between understanding the importance of listening and making a conscious effort to actually listen.

Listening to others and showing them that you have listened creates incredibly positive perceptions in their minds. Human nature is such that we like to be listened to. We warm towards those who appear to listen to us and appear to show interest in our ideas and feelings. Conversely, we shun those who appear more interested in the sound of their own voice and who appear disinterested in our opinions and points of view. As leaders, we need to ask more questions and give fewer opinions. Two ears and one mouth, used in that proportion.

If it sounds overly simple, then do not be fooled. Most of us believe that we are good listeners. Most of us are not.

Listening to people is essential to engage them emotionally. By making a conscious effort to listen and demonstrating that you have heard what they said, you can begin to assess their desires and work with them to develop their ideas. This empowers them, motivates them, and sometimes inspires them to do good things and when they produce good outcomes, you need to recognize their achievements. Recognition is an incredibly powerful motivator.

Listen,
Engage emotionally and,
Assess their desire then,
Develop their ideas,
Empower them to act,
Recognize.

LEADER.

My apologies! I just added an acronym to the recipe.

Chapter Four

Don't Push a Car with a Rope

I cannot leave the subject of listening without going into more detail otherwise, there is a danger that what I mean by listening to people and engaging them emotionally may not be fully understood.

If your car has broken down and the engine has decided not to run, you may decide to push it. Many of us have been in that situation where you try pushing the car and you meet with resistance. Pushing a car is hard work progress is very slow. We may decide that the effort involved is too much and give up. What we need is a tow. We need to attach the rope to the broken-down vehicle and pull it to wherever it needs to be to get it fixed. Pulling it is faster and easier than pushing it. If the car represents a problem at work and the repair shop is the goal or the destination then the rope represents listening. Things happen more efficiently, more effectively and with more velocity when we show others that we are listening to them. Listening to people is to pull them along as opposed to pushing them by telling them what to do. Pushing people builds resistance and slows you down. Pulling people gains you momentum. They don't resist their own ideas.

Listening involves so much more than simply using our ears. To listen to the opinions of others you may have to initially use your mouth to ask a question. Once the question has been asked and you start listening to the answer, you must make a conscious effort to show people that you are listening to them to influence their perceptions of you in a positive way. Check your understanding with them even if you already fully understood what they said. By repeating back to them what they had previously told you, it shows to them that you were really listening to them and that you are interested in what they have to say. This resonates with them on a subconscious level and on the Feeling/Attitude level they warm towards you. They like you.

I have no intention of making this section a chapter on listening skills, as most of us have already been there and eaten a portion at the training and development cafeteria. It is important however for you to remember what you learned there and to put it into practice in order to become competent at asking open questions and encouraging others to talk. One of my favorite techniques is the use of reflective questions. It's something I learned on a training course at Xerox UK back in the eighties and it has proven to be invaluable. Asking reflective questions simply requires you to wait until the speaker seems to be finished speaking and then you repeat their last few words back to them with a question mark or inflection in your voice. For example, if someone would say, "This is much more difficult than it used to be," you would respond inquisitively by asking, "More difficult than it used to be?" or even simply by saying, "More difficult?" By asking a reflective question and pausing afterwards, the speaker perceives you to be listening and is prompted to go further and explain more about what they were saying. It is amazing how long you can hold a conversation with someone by asking only reflective questions without them realizing that you are doing nothing more than this.

I remember clearly on that course that I attended when the idea was introduced to me and my seven Xerox colleagues. We were staying at the Xerox UK residential training center, which in those days was in Newport Pagnall, Buckinghamshire in Southern England. One of my fellow course members lived only five minutes away, so each evening he would return home to his family while the remainder of us stayed and either worked in our rooms or relaxed in the bar area.

The day after we were introduced to reflective questions, our locally based colleague arrived in the classroom that morning, all excited to tell us about his use of the reflective technique from the previous evening. He had gone home to find his wife in the kitchen, already preparing dinner. He walked in and asked her how her day had been. She responded to him and when she was almost finished speaking, he reflected her last few words back to her while he joined in with the work and helped prepare the meal and set the table places. He said that she would talk and go into more details and that as she would begin to verbally dry up, he reflected her last few words to her with an inquisitive tone in his voice. Each time that he did this she continued to go into greater detail or take off on another subject. After almost half an hour of reflection and listening, his wife said to him as they sat down to eat, "This is the best conversation we've had in years."

What happened in this simple example is much more significant than merely listening and finding out the details about his wife's day and her interaction with her friends and colleagues. By showing interest and by using her own words to show her that he was really listening, he succeeded in connecting with her emotionally. It was significant enough for her to consciously realize that she was enjoying a conversation with her husband in a way that was better than usual. This small example shows that even listening just a little can be emotionally uplifting, so imagine what can be achieved if we make a conscious effort to listen a lot. The more that we can show people that we are truly listening to them and that we understand how they feel, the easier it is to be able to connect with them emotionally. As this emotional connection develops, they start to feel more comfortable with us and mutual trust begins to develop that gradually allows them to share even more information with us. The more they tell us how they feel about anything and everything the closer we get to their desires, and we improve our chances or increase our opportunities to inspire them.

Measurable Management® refers to this listening and involving approach as "The Pull Style" of leadership and if it does not already come naturally to you, it can only be developed with practice, lots, and lots of practice.

The truth is that many of us think that we are better at listening and involving than we really are. If you have ever watched the TV show "American Idol" and listened to the auditions, it is amazing how some people clearly believe that they have a talent for singing when the talent is completely nonexistent. Their belief is based on years of positive reinforcement from doting parents and grandparents who have told them from being little toddlers that they are Awesome! Eventually they delude themselves that they are truly awesome and then they go on TV and make a ridiculous spectacle of themselves before walking away from the audition ranting about the stupidity of Simon Cowell and his cohort for not recognizing their awesomeness.

I often see a less extreme version of this craziness when we take people through the group meetings and group activities contained within the Measurable Management® Program. As we discuss the importance of listening and the need to make a conscious effort to demonstrate that they have listened, they will sit there with their heads nodding in agreement. We will then involve them in a group exercise where there is an opportunity for them to do more listening than talking. However, instead of listening and using the Pull Style that they agreed minutes previously was the appropriate style to use, they will instantly revert to type and start Pushing. People who use the Push style do more talking than listening, they give orders and instructions as they propose their own solutions and interrupt others. From a Thinking point of view, we see them as aggressive or authoritarian. On the Feeling level, they make us uncomfortable; they might even annoy us or make us angry and resentful. From the Willing point of view, motivation levels are extremely low; it is impossible for them to be anything other than low. Remember we said earlier that we do not really need to be trained in how to motivate people if only we would just stop doing things that de-motivate them. Push style, when used constantly, de-motivates people.

When the head nodders have finished slapping their foreheads in frustration with themselves, the program takes them through more discussions and exercises that really do begin to change their behaviors and we see much more pulling than pushing and gradually the forehead-slapping disappears altogether.

I am not saying that we should never use the Push Style. In fact, we need to be confidant and comfortable with using Push techniques when short time scales and emergency situations call for it. We do need to, however, use the Pull style much more frequently than the Push style if we want to keep people motivated and increase the velocity of positive change. The more frequently that you Pull people the less frequently you need to Push them.

CHAPTER FIVE

BIG ILLUSIONS SMALL TRUTHS

(The Organic Manager)

Quite a few years ago, I went to see a performance by the world-famous illusionist David Copperfield. I love to be entertained by people who can create the illusion of being able to do phenomenal things. Copperfield is world famous for his often-stunning illusions not least of which is the one that seems to make the Statue of Liberty disappear from New York Harbor.

Another well-known illusionist, Criss Angel, amazed his audiences at the Luxor Hotel in Las Vegas with his apparent ability to levitate and even walk across the swimming pool.

David Blaine survived 63 hours (about 2 and a half days) in full view of the public encased in a block of ice in New York City's Times Square. Such feats would truly be phenomenal if they were a reality, but the three aforementioned people are all illusionists and are proud to admit it.

A great illusion leaves you amazed and saying things like "I can't begin to imagine how they did that." That statement alone says a lot about the imagination of the illusionist. Sometimes the imagination involved in creating the illusion can be as creative and phenomenal as the feat that they are trying to make you believe in. As entertaining as these illusions are, they are just illusions, and the performers make no claims to the contrary and the audience knows it is not real, but the fascination lies in "How did they do that"? Are these performers capable of thinking like da Vinci? Who knows?

I have visited many organizations that are good at creating illusions, and like many illusions, the deception begins as soon as you enter the building. Over the many years that I have spent helping organizations to increase the velocity at which they make things happen and improve their performance, I have sat in dozens of reception areas while waiting for the CEO or whoever my appointment is with to come and greet me. As I wait, I look around and take note of my surroundings. Reception areas within organizations are often remarkably similar. It is quite common to see that the walls are dressed in certificates or accolades and awards from vendors or the Chamber of Commerce and other professional bodies. Lines of certificates showing compliance with ISO 9001 or some such quality standard, a popular one in the UK, is a dark blue plaque announcing to everyone that the organization is an accredited Investor in People. There are Quality Awards, Customer Service Awards, Health & Safety Certificates and sometimes recognition for acts of philanthropy and framed letters of gratitude. Usually what these trophies are doing is sending a message to all visitors that we are good people to do business with.

The Customer Service Awards are supposed to let us know that they are customer-focused and that things are done with the customer in mind.

The Quality Awards and Compliance Certificates are there to reassure the visitor that the organization has great products and that their goods and services are reliable and superior.

The Health & Safety awards and Philanthropic recognitions are there to let everyone know that People come before Profit and that we are the Good Guys. It is really nothing more than a marketing exercise that is designed to create an impression or illusion about the organization from the moment the visitor enters the building.

I am not being a cynic and I do not want to imply that everything is deliberately designed to deceive the public with smoke and mirrors. I applaud the attempts of organizations to improve their processes, their health and safety records and for giving back to the community. It is just that I have learned from experience that what we see in the reception is often a big **illusion based on some small truths.** I am also very aware of the importance of accreditation as a means of recognizing the organization's ability to meet and maintain standards that allow you to stay in business.

Iowa City Fire Department used Measurable Management® to help them do just that by working towards accreditation with the Commission on Fire Accreditation International. In addition to achieving their accreditation, they also used the program to improve the health, safety, and fitness of dept personnel, develop an officer growth and improvement program as well as improve the evaluation and marketing of fire protection services.

They really made an impact on their people and on their community and if they were in the business of decorating receptions rather than saving lives, they would have ticked all the boxes in the reception decoration department. In 2011 Iowa City Fire Dept nominated Robin Byrne's Measurable Management for the United Nations NGO Positive Peace Award.

As I recall my early days in management working for Xerox in the UK. I went on my first Leadership Through Quality initiative in 1983, long before most other organizations in the UK became aware of Total Quality Management and within a couple of years, I believed that we had become a customer-focused organization. The reality which is far easier for me to recognize today with the benefit of hindsight, is that although Xerox UK at that time were much more customer-focused than many others, they were still primarily a sales-driven organization. Much of what we were doing in a Total Quality or Customer Satisfaction sense was also doing much to provide ammunition for our sales and marketing departments as it was for our customers, which is OK, but I know that back then, not everyone was aligned behind the customer.

I am not blaming organizations for marketing themselves in this way I am simply stating that many, if not most, are exceptionally good at talking the talk, but when you move from the reception to behind the scenes, there is not as much tangible evidence that these organizations are walking the walk. It is not because they do not want to, it is usually because they do not know how to. Some know that they don't know, but many more do not know that they don't know. They do not know their own reality. They see certification and accreditation as proof of a quality or a customer-focused approach to doing business.

The truth is that the only proof of being customer-focused lies with your customers and not with accrediting bodies. How much repeat business do you get from your customers and how many referrals do your customers make to others? If as much effort went into truly satisfying the needs of our core customers as we put into marketing our goods and services, we would do so much better.

Fred Reicheld, in his book "The Ultimate Question," claims that the only question that matters is to ask customers, "How happy would you be to recommend our products and services to a friend or colleague?"

He talks about improving your NPS or Net Promoter Score and that by increasing the ratio of promoters to detractors you will significantly improve your bottom line.

He is right in this statement and organizations that are able to improve their NPS will certainly improve from Lousy to Mediocre or Mediocre to Good or Good to Great, but not much further. This approach is lacking something if you want to get your organization into The da Vinci Zone if you want to transcend your perceived limitations.

It is good to move from the illusion of customer focus to walking the walk and truly becoming customer-focused.

Think about those certificates hanging on the reception walls for just a moment. They do not just promote your focus on Customer Service; they also promote your regard for your employees and your communities. Focusing on the customer is good and if you improve your NPS you will certainly increase your margins by more points than your NPS increased. If, however, you can simultaneously do positive things for your employees and your community, you will soar like an eagle. Organizations that do this grow organically with little need for advertising fertilizers or marketing pesticides. Just as organic farmers apply different farming techniques to grow healthy thriving crops, business leaders need to adopt organic leadership methods to grow healthy and thriving businesses.

Remember when we said in Chapter 1 that organizations are organic because they are made up of people? The employees are people, the customers are people, and the suppliers are people. **People-focused organizations thrive while product-focused organizations dive.**

Organizations that focus on measuring production figures, sales figures, marketing demographics, ROI and the gazillion other measurements that obsess them become stuck in a rut of product-focused, sales-driven production and **the only difference between a rut and a grave is the depth.**

If you are genuinely serious about moving away from being merely an illusion of a great organization to truly becoming a great organization capable of Giant Leaps, how do you do that? How do you become an organic leader?

The answer lies in the title of this chapter. You need to move from illusion to inclusion. You need to remember what we said in the chapter entitled "The Oh Shit Syndrome" and recognize that leadership, decision making and problem-solving are not the exclusive domain of the management team. Stop using nonorganic leadership methods and start developing Organic Leaders. The workforce, our customers and our communities are fertile ground, and we need to start plowing and planting in these areas.

We need to involve our people, our customers, and our communities in such an open way that they take ownership of the problems. We need to involve them and encourage them to develop the solutions because when they own the solution, they do not resist the implementation. When resistance is minimal or nonexistent, conflicts disappear and things begin to change very rapidly, Giant Leaps become a possibility.

When products and services improve, word-of-mouth marketing becomes immensely powerful because, among other things, Net Promoter Scores increase, even if you have never heard of them and do not even measure them. When Health & Safety standards improve and morale levels rise, attrition levels fall and so do the costs that are associated with attrition. Recruitment becomes easier and less expensive because everyone wants to work for your organization. When you give to your communities, they give back. The give back with loyalty, whether it be customer loyalty or employee loyalty. They give back with gratitude that satisfies workers and makes them feel proud to work for a caring organization. They like being the Good Guys. It makes the organization an even greater place to work. Doing more positive things not just for your customers but also for your employees and your communities brings you so much closer to the da Vinci Zone. It makes you a more organic leader; it brings much more significant growth; and it helps you to sow the seeds so that you may eventually reap the harvest.

Chapter Six

The Arsonist and The Fire Fighter?

It is an interesting and conflicting combination, isn't it? The criminal arsonist and the hero firefighter. Two absolute opposites with completely opposing objectives, one with good intentions and the other with bad. One trying to incinerate everything, the other trying to save us from incineration.

Although they have opposing objectives, for each of them to achieve their objectives and produce successful outcomes, they both must be good at precisely the same three things. This is also true of any individual in any kind of organization that you care to identify. For a person or an organization to successfully achieve an objective and produce a desired outcome or result, they all do the same three things. It makes no difference if you are performing brain surgery or collecting trash, the success or failure of your endeavor will depend on how well you manage these three things.

All organizations are different and the markets or

communities in which they operate are also radically different. This leads training companies to believe that they have a competitive edge if they produce bespoke training programs to specifically meet the needs of that organization. I have read on dozens of training company and consulting company websites that the differences between organizations make it impossible to meet the training and development needs of every single company with an off-the-shelf, non-bespoke product. They boast that every one of their programs is uniquely developed for that client and is, therefore, 100% appropriate for them.

Smoke and mirrors… It might be true that the program they develop for you is not exactly identical to the program developed for the organization across the street, but in all likelihood, it will be a re-hash of what they are good at, dressed a little differently to create the illusion that it was all done from scratch, especially for you. Let us head back to the HR Cafeteria. If they were manufacturing custom dinner services, every plate might have your unique design on it, but it is the same basic plate that everyone else has—it holds the same amount of food and functions just like everyone else's dinner plate. You have simply been upsold.

The illusion is that they think that they are customer-focused when in truth, they are product-focused and are using moderate customization to market their goods and services. They are focused on the customer, but primarily, they are focused on their products and their profits. They may not, however, even believe this themselves. They may believe that they are really trying to satisfy differing client requirements, but they have not really understood the meaning of customer focus. This lack of understanding has influenced their perceptions of their own reality. They investigate the needs of the customer, but they are drawn back to their own products and services like a magnet and try to make what they are capable of fit what the customer is asking for. They then try and sell the solution instead of having a solution that sells itself. Most organizations who passionately believe that they are truly customer focused are not. They have deluded themselves into a false understanding of their own reality. Much as I did when I worked for Xerox, and we were the first-ever recipients of the "EFQM" Award (European Foundation for Quality Management) and in the USA "The Malcolm Baldridge Award." As previously said, we were more customer-focused than most, but we were even more focused on business outcomes. These awards were well publicized and found their way onto the walls of our reception areas in all our branches and offices world-wide. The intentions were good, but we still used a little smoke and the occasional mirror.

Now if all organizations fundamentally do the same three things to achieve a successful outcome, then imagine an off-the-shelf solution that makes every organization regardless of size, sector, or service better at doing those three things. This must be a better value proposition than paying for needless customization. If in doing so, it also generates ROI far greater than the costs of implementation, this must be a value proposition that sells itself. This is where Measurable Management demonstrates why it is not only in The da Vinci Zone but how it will help you to get your organization into the Zone also. This is about to become one of those unique moments of realization that many refer to as an Aha Moment.

To achieve a successful outcome for any objective, large or small, we all do the same three things and here they are.

We manage our **resources**; we manage the **relationships** between the people who are essential to making it happen and we control or manage the **processes** that make it happen. It is that simple. That is all that you do. At any one time while you are at work you have your hands on one or more of those three things. There is nothing else. If something should go wrong, as we all know it does from time to time and we are able to pinpoint exactly what caused our unplanned or unexpected outcome, we will always find the problem to be either a Resource, Relationship or Process related problem. There really is nowhere else for it to sit. This is what we do whenever we manage or implement anything at work. We might be a hospital or an Air Force, a car plant, or a hotel. Whatever type of goods or services that we provide, to provide them successfully we must manage our resources, manage our relationships, and control our processes. An organic leader who understands this simple truth, can therefore adapt amazingly quickly to managing operations in an organization that may be completely alien to them at the outset. A systematic approach to evaluating these three areas and relating them to our organizations two or three Key Issues will have a dramatic and positive effect on the success of those Key Issues or Strategic Objectives

Measurable Management® is such a program. It has already been implemented by an enormous variety of organizations, from city governments to family-owned businesses, from armed forces to hospitals, from manufacturing companies to service based not for profits and from Europe to Africa to the USA.

By drawing its real content from the individual's job the program becomes self-customizing. By having everyone evaluate the resources that they use daily, the relationships that they are involved in daily and the processes that they put their hands on every day, the program draws its actual content from the participant's job. This drawing of content makes it 100% relevant to every participant, regardless of their role or position in the organization. It also makes it 100% relevant to every organization no matter what they do, how they do it or who they do it with. Schools and local government have improved their performance using this approach with as much success as more obviously business-related organizations.

I remember that we agreed to run a Measurable Management Program with Darlington and Durham Fire and Rescue in the Northeast of England. They were convinced that customization would be necessary as, in their mind's firefighting, was radically different from running a business. I did not argue, but I suggested that we initially run with a non-customized pilot program to determine what level of customization would be required. My suggestion was accepted, and we proceeded with the traditional non-customized program. The outcomes were so exceptionally good that they asked us not to change a thing.

When we visit the Measurable Management Cafeteria, every plate, bowl, pot, pan, knife, fork, spoon, chopstick is always from the same matching set. It is the food on the plate that is unique. Unique to you. Created and served up by your very own in-house Michelin Star chefs who provided the ingredients themselves to deliver a feast of benefits that will contradict the old proverb and prove that you cannot have too many cooks.

This approach is simple and can be implemented virtually instantly. Participants systematically look at Resources, Relationships and Processes with the Key Business Issues or Objectives in mind and take note of anything at all that they feel has an opportunity for improvement. Let me use a real-life example to demonstrate the simplicity of this approach.

(Resources) I facilitated a Program with a company in the UK that manufactured dehumidifiers and were looking to improve productivity as one of their Key Issues. One of the team leaders working through the program listed the resources that he and his team use daily. I asked him to pick out one at random and he chose an air gun that they use on the manufacturing lines to fasten screws and tighten bolts.

I asked him how satisfied he was with the air gun. Did it do the job for which it was designed and intended to be used for?

He replied that that it was excellent and then after a short pause, he commented that, "We just don't have enough of them." Naturally, I invited him to expand on the latter comment. "Well," he went on to say, "sometimes we have to go looking for one because someone from another line has borrowed ours and not returned it."

"How frequently does this happen"? I asked, "and what do you do about it"?

"Every day," he replied, "sometimes two or three times a day and we spend 10 minutes or more each time either looking for it or waiting for the other line to finish with it."

"What happens to your line while you are looking for the air gun?"

"It stops! Production is held up until we find it and re-connect it to our line."

You do not have to be da Vinci to see where this is leading. Hours of costly downtime and lost production per year with costs per unit rising as we continue to pay workers while they fail to produce. Potentially unhappy customers as delivery deadlines fail to be adhered to. Expensive payments in overtime to make up for lost time and all for the need of an extra air gun or two.

(Processes) "Interesting"! I commented. "Can you describe what you do with the air gun? In other words, describe the process that this resource is applied to."

He went on to describe the process and when he finished describing it, I asked him if it always ran smoothly, or if anything occasionally went wrong.

He said that it worked well for the most part, except that sometimes they would hook it up and go to use it only to discover that they were out of compressed air and needed to change the bottle.

"Does that happen often and when it does what do you have to do?"

I will not bore you with the obvious, but you can easily see how improvements to the process of supplying compressed air, checking the supply levels, and making sure backup supplies are available would have big process improvements and impact even more positively on production efficiency.

(Relationships) Finally, I asked him to write down some of the words that he would use to describe the relationship conditions between the people on the line who had their hands on this process. Was there an atmosphere of mutual trust, cooperation, and friendliness or one of suspicion or hostility in their relationships with each other?

I noted that he had written the word "cynicism" and asked him to explain further. He started talking about the negative behavior of one team member who consistently resisted ideas to improve things and constantly criticized management for trying to make them work harder.

I asked if the behavior of this individual had any negative effect on teamwork and productivity and of course, he answered in the affirmative.

It is very easy to see how looking at each of our resources and evaluating them in simple terms of how the user feels about the resource, the process that the resource is applied to and the relationships between those that have their hands on the process, can quickly and easily identify a significant number of ideas for action. While this may look like something that you already do, it is the structured approach of breaking it down into the only three areas that matter and applying the listening and involving Pull Style to the implementation of change, that makes it "unnervingly simple yet powerfully effective."

Of course you do not have to start with a resource. You may have issues with a process or a relationship and if you consider all three areas, it does not really matter which one comes first.

The title of this chapter now makes perfect sense. If I am an arsonist or a firefighter, I will be a much better arsonist or firefighter if I simply pay attention to my resources, relationships, and processes. If you think back over the last few weeks or months at work and pick on one or two things that did not go as planned and evaluate what went wrong. It will always be a resource, a relationship or a process or a combination of two or more of those areas that hold the root cause of the problem. There is nowhere else. Everything and I really do mean everything, that you do at work revolves around your resources, your relationships, and your processes. The organic team leader only needs to start asking more questions and refraining from offering solutions to get your employees, your very own in-house consultants/gourmet chefs, to develop and thereby take ownership of their own solutions that they will be able to implement without negative conflict, without stressful coercion and without resistance.

It all sounds amazingly easy, and it can be, but the reality is that easy to understand is not always easy to implement. Sometimes the simple changes can be exceedingly difficult to implement and changing the leadership culture of an organization inevitably means changing behaviors. Behaviors are difficult to change because they have become habits and habits are hard to break. It takes time, it takes a concentrated effort, and it takes repetition. It is ok to fail, and it is ok to make mistakes. Not trying to change, however, is not ok.

As children, we learn to ride bikes by falling off them a few times and we learn to avoid hot surfaces by getting burned. Even da Vinci made errors. To begin to get it right first time, you may frequently get it wrong at your previous attempts. Only a small number of da Vinci paintings exist because he was a procrastinator. I can only imagine how many pages he would have screwed up because he failed to meet his own high standards. It is important, however, to avoid analysis paralysis and implement your plans. Even if you do not get it right first time, it is OK to get it right the second time, as long as you eventually get it right.

To move towards the Zone, you must make a move.

CHAPTER SEVEN
TAPPING INTO THE CIA

The title of this chapter all sounds very James Bond, but obviously, we will not be breaking into CIA headquarters in Langley, VA and bugging the place. The CIA mentioned in this chapter title is simply an acronym to help us remember the three basic elements for getting into The da Vinci Zone.

Creativity
Inventiveness
Artistry

Remember that in Chapter One, "Think Like da Vinci," we said that these three areas were the very qualities that da Vinci possessed and excelled in. It would be foolish to think that we can develop our workforce to be as creative, inventive, or artistic as da Vinci, but everyone can possess these qualities to greater or lesser degrees. It would be more foolish of us not to explore these qualities and attempt to develop those talents. We do not know what hidden talents exist within a group of people unless we present them with opportunities to use and display those talents.

I love to use the analogy that everyone in the organization is like an unexplored attic. If you search through enough attics, you will find a few treasures. Sometimes we need others to help us look because we cannot always recognize a treasure when we see it. Indeed, I was surprised to learn that da Vinci received an informal education in Latin, geometry and mathematics but did not show any particular signs of aptitude, **his teachers could not see the treasure sitting right under their noses.**

We need to search through the attics. The more we blow away the dust and the cobwebs, the more we discover. Eventually if we look long enough and search hard enough, we may find a Rembrandt in the attic or even a da Vinci. By exploring the hidden talents of the workforce, we sometimes uncover something of such value that we did not even know we had. Measurable Management provides a structure and a proven process that helps you search through the attic and then it provides you with an art gallery to display your treasures.

There is an obvious link between Creativity, Inventiveness and Artistry and the three things that we talked about in the previous chapter. Resources, Relationships and Processes, the three things that we all manage and control to achieve an outcome.

Being **creative** and being **resourceful** are terribly similar. Using your creativity to maximize the use of existing resources can enable you to do more with less.

Doing more with less, is an excellent quality to have in times of cutbacks and cost control; indeed, doing more with less at any time will more than likely gain you a competitive advantage in terms of your pricing or profitability. There is no better example of this that I can think of than the amazing creativity and resourcefulness displayed by the team of scientists who worked to save the lives of the Apollo 13 crew.

Apollo 13 was to be the third mission to land on the Moon. An explosion in one of the oxygen tanks crippled the spacecraft during flight and forced the crew to orbit the Moon and return to the Earth without landing. As a result of these occurrences, the Command Module was powered down and the Lunar Landing Module was configured to supply the necessary power and other consumables to keep the crew alive. All Landing Module systems performed satisfactorily in providing the necessary power and environmental control to the spacecraft except for the ability to remove carbon dioxide from the spacecraft's atmosphere. The Landing Module cartridges alone would not satisfy the total requirement and if a solution was not found to enable the round hoses from the Landing Module to fit the square cartridges from the Command Module, then the crew would surely die of carbon monoxide poisoning long before they returned to Earth.

The Apollo 13 Crew the day before the launch
Source www.awesomestories.com
James A. Lovell, John L. Swigert & Fred W Haise Jr.

The scientists at NASA gathered the resources that they knew were available to the crew on Apollo 13 and using plastic bags, duct tape and torn-up flight manuals, they devised a way to make a square peg fit a round hole. The crew, with direction from Mission Control, built the adapter for the Command Module cartridges to accept the Landing Module hoses and the CO^2 levels immediately began to fall. This is a wonderful example of how when you "bathe" in the "Creativity Pool" the resourcefulness of people can create a phenomenal result.

This example also highlights what was said in Chapter 1 regarding how some people get into the Zone more frequently than others. NASA did it to complete the challenge laid down by JFK in 1961 and nine years later in 1970, they returned to the Zone and began to think like da Vinci to save the lives of the Apollo 13 crew.

We expect the smart people to be in the Zone all, or most of the time but if that were the case, then perhaps Apollo 13 would never have had an explosion in the first place.

If Creativity and Managing Resources are strongly linked so must Inventiveness and Developing Processes be linked. So, what is the difference? Aren't Creativity and Inventiveness the same thing? No, not quite.

Creativity is the pathway to invention. In other words, resourcefulness and imagination will help us to be able to change the process and improve the outcome. The new process and the improved outcome are the inventions that have been developed from our creativity and our resourcefulness. Gathering the unrelated objects together that lay around the spacecraft stimulated creative thought. Physically putting them together, failing and trying another approach eventually turned that creativity into a solution, an invention that worked. Creativity alone might only result in chaos; inventiveness starts to bring order to the chaos and solutions to the table. Some people are highly likely to be highly creative and able to generate unique ideas, others are highly inventive and can seize on those ideas and build on them to turn that idea into a workable solution, an improvement, or as in this case a lifesaving CO^2 processor.

Leonardo da Vinci possessed all these amazing qualities in one mind and these qualities also exist to varying degrees within individual organizations. Remember how we talked about organizations being organic and that we need to try and think of the people within the organization as the mind/brain? All we need to do is open the shut valves in the mind/brain of the organization to allow that creativity and inventiveness to flow and that is where the Artistry becomes essential.

As Creativity is to Resources and Inventiveness is to Processes Artistry is to Relationships.

Getting things done through others is the very essence of being a leader and yet, if not managed with finesse, it can create as many problems as it solves. It is a strange thought, isn't it that management can be artistic? But it is artistic and recognizing that there is an artistry to leading and influencing the behavior of others begins to move you away from conventional management thinking to thinking like da Vinci. It moves you towards The da Vinci Zone.

How do you get others to do what you want them to do when you want it done and in the way that you want it done?

Since strangling is not an option and yelling and bullying might not create long-term loyalty and will definitely de-motivate people, we need to think about the artistry of leadership.

Sure, you can just tell someone to do something, and they will do it just because the boss told them to do it. If they do not jump to it and do it in a timely manner, we can raise our voices and tell them to do it NOW! And they may do it. We may even have to threaten them with some kind of negative reinforcement if they do not get it done to get them to produce the result and finally satisfy our needs. These techniques all sit squarely in the Push Style and have little to do with artistry. These are the behaviors that de-motivate the already motivated.

Some people manage and lead others this way daily and think that they are good leaders because they still manage to get the job done even if "according to them," their team is "a lazy bunch of cynics."

What this manager either does not hear or fails to listen to are the grumbles of the individual doing the task. They often seem critical of what they are being asked to do because they feel it is not what it should be. They say things like, "This is dumb," or "Who on earth thought this was a smart idea?" They are the ones with their hands on the day-to-day processes that have evolved out of the creativity or lack of creativity and inventiveness of others. They know what is wrong and often, by applying their own creativity and inventiveness, they know how to fix it. The problem lies in the lack of artistry within team leaders and managers to encourage these ideas. When we tell people what to do, we adopt the Push style of leadership and we find ourselves shutting off the valves in the mind when we should be opening them up by developing the Pull style, the listening and involving style of leadership.

According to the section in Measurable Management® entitled "Influencing Behavior," the most obvious difference between being a leader and a non-leader is the reliance on getting things done through other people.

How does the Push style manager get things done when they rely on the cooperation of other departments, and they do not have the authority to tell them to just do it? More intriguingly, how do they influence the behavior of someone who is positioned above them in the organization and get them to do something that they might not otherwise want to do?

In my book "Cultural Change Through Measurable Management," I recall watching TV in England one evening when an advert for Army recruitment came on and caught my attention. The camera represented the eyes of the Army officer as he approached an angry group of rebels with his patrol. The rebel leader looked like a ruthless individual and he shouted and yelled, waving his automatic weapon as the British Officer and his men approached. The voiceover commentary asked, "If you were this officer, how would you get this man to share his water with you and your troop"? At that moment, the officer removed his sunglasses and the commentary continued with, "Making eye contact is the first step in showing that you are listening to someone and reducing conflict levels."

The officer in this situation really must influence the behavior of someone who is outside of his direct control. Not only does the rebel leader not want to cooperate, but he is also dangerously hostile and a real potential threat to safety. Push style could lead to a bloodbath and cause injury or even death to one or more of the officer's own men. Situations like this call for artistry.

We may have great creativity and inventiveness but without the artistry of leadership, it will lead to nowhere. To lead others, we need to have the artistic skills to motivate, instruct, support, develop and communicate with others. It is from within this skill set that truly outstanding leaders emerge. These are precisely the skills that inspirational leaders like JFK and Winston Churchill possessed. These are the skills that inspire people to reach beyond their perceived limitations and attempt to do the phenomenal. This is the Artistry of Leadership.

Given the importance of implementation, and the need to overcome resistance to the execution of our plans, it has always surprised me that organizations always spend time and money on initiatives that produce ideas for improvement and only bolt on as an afterthought the development of leadership and team building. This usually only happens when the results of their endeavors are not as good as they were originally expecting.

The Measurable Management® solution is completely the reverse of this traditional approach. It is essential to first develop the listening and involving style, the artistry of leadership, and then apply it to a teamwork approach to problem-solving. **Great art is inspired and from great art, others gain inspiration.** If we influence people in an effective way, engaging with them emotionally and igniting their desires, they too will be inspired to do excellent work and when we are surrounded by exacting standards, it influences us in a positive way. Naturally therefore, as we have learned that behavior begets behavior, it is a logical assumption that bad leaders were very probably led badly. Most people led by gang leaders never develop the more subtle skills to lead but they often develop "lead poisoning." A Rut and a Grave perhaps?

Develop a listening and involving style of leadership first and embed this before you rush into creating solutions and forcing them onto people. Open the stop valves. If team leaders do not develop this approach, then you can forget tapping into the CIA. The first 50% of every Measurable Management® Initiative is spent developing this approach the second 50% is spent applying it to the implementation of ideas. By taking this approach, you will engage the team and open a stop valve or two. You may be amazed at how many Rembrandts and other valuable treasures you will find.

Chapter Eight
Swimming Up Waterfalls

I have lost count of the number of times that someone has raised with me the question of sustainability. In fact, I have been asked this question so many times that I started to think about why is it such a frequently asked question?

It does not take much thinking to come to the realization that everyone asking the question is doing so because they have run into difficulties sustaining other initiatives. The flavor of the month was initially met and embraced with enthusiasm but a year or two later, there seems to be a drudgery attached that is making it difficult to sustain. The response to their question therefore, should be, "Why do you ask?" If you ask that question, then you are practicing the Pull Style and if you really listen to the answers, you will begin to engage with that person emotionally. Like the patient speaking to the doctor, they will tell you of their Total Quality aches and their Lean Sigma pains, their EOS uncomfortable traction, or their lack of equilibrium on the unbalanced Scorecard. They will tell you about their early successes, the gradual drop in enthusiasm, and the now stubborn resistance.

It is hard to sustain if it feels like a pain.

If you are having problems with sustaining an existing initiative, then you are having a problem with motivation. If you are having a problem with motivation, you are having a problem with leadership. Remember that people start out motivated and leaders de-motivate them. We de-motivate people when we impose ideas and solutions onto them. In most cases, they are resisting the flavor of the month initiative because it lost its flavor and now, they are being force-fed.

I mentioned in the chapter entitled Corporate Constipation that "Continual Improvement even sounds slow and as it never has a finish line, it can seem a little de-motivational." Continuous Improvement is essential but **swimming up waterfalls meets with resistance.**

People want to feel what it is like to cross the finish line and achieve something that genuinely is "enormously satisfying and gloriously inspirational." This inspires the desire to experience it repeatedly.

You cannot sustain a steady pace if you are running in and endless race.

This is why diets often do not work! Too many "Flavor of the Month" initiatives are introduced to put the organization onto a diet. We even use the terminology,

"Lean and Mean" as we regularly consult our Jenny Craig or South Beach black belts. We go to our process improvement Weight Watcher meetings and step on the scales to measure our success. We lose some weight but after a while, we become tired of the daily diet of condensed initiative soup and we long for a burger, more than that we desire it and as desires are much stronger than wants, we eventually succumb to our desires. Gradually the waistline once more expands and no longer fits the new slimmer corporate wardrobe, so we look for the next flavor of the month to get our weight watchers back on the corporate Lean machine.

Measurable Management is completely effortless because it changes behavior permanently. Leaders who consistently involve their teams, remove the pain and replace it with pleasure, and those things that give us pleasure become hard to resist.

Remove the pains, enjoy the gains!

The Acronym I introduced earlier L E A D E R Listen, Engage, Assess, Develop, Empower, Reward, makes sense if you do everything and make sure that you do not forget to reward. Reward and Recognition is a huge part of motivation and sustainability. It reinforces the emotional connection to people. Recognizing the efforts of people in a public way rather than a one-on-one pat on the back approach will motivate them much more than a financial bonus in the Christmas paycheck although that is also nice.

We know that people want to do an excellent job, but what they really want is for everyone else to know that they do an excellent job. It must be the right form of authentic recognition though. All too often, we see a kid get pulled off the field or the basketball court and we will hear the coach say, "Good Job Son." They say it to soften the blow of being substituted for their mediocrity and it's used so often that it has lost the original hardness of its authentic meaning. **So often** translates into **soften**.

Saying "Good Job" has almost become meaningless, but it's clearly less de-motivational than saying "Lousy Job". Telling others however that "Dave really did a great job" and telling them this in front of Dave will have a much more significant effect on Dave's motivation. He may be a little embarrassed but underneath the red flush to the face, there will be a straight flush of pride. Pride is felt in the heart, pride warms the spirit and the difference between motivation and inspiration is that spiritual and emotional connection.

Recognizing the work of others or the contribution that they make creates good perceptions of you in their minds, this in turn fosters positive attitudes towards you and results in positive behavior. They have no choice; it happens as sure as night follows day. If you want to sustain good behaviors, then you must publicly recognize and reward people. Feed their desire do not put them on a Lean diet of anonymity.

To aspire to do phenomenal things should become our desire because if, by reaching for that desire we are able to perform far beyond our perceived best, then we are transcending perceived limitations and are reaching toward The da Vinci Zone.

CHAPTER NINE

ALIGNMENT OR MALIGNANT?

There is much talk about the alignment of the organization and the necessity for leadership teams to be in alignment to achieve our objectives more easily and transform our organizations more effectively. My good friend Miles Kierson is considered by many to be the expert in Executive Team Alignment and authored the book, *The Transformational Power of Executive Team Alignment*. Miles lives in Chicago and has worked with the Senior Leadership Teams of many Fortune Companies.

The work of Miles Kierson at the executive level aligns very nicely with the Measurable Management® Program. When he saw what Measurable Management® is and how it works, he realized that—in his own words—"I had found the missing link I had been looking for in my work: the bridge between my own initial focus with clients (creating the foundation for being successful in some organization-wide initiative or strategic implementation) and being successful at the implementation of what got created in that period I call formulation." In other words,

Miles was highly successful at getting SLTs or Senior Leadership Teams to align behind the organization's Key Issues and Objectives and saw in Measurable Management® the perfect vehicle for continuing that alignment with the rest of the organization.

If the SLT is not aligned the journey will take longer. If the organization is a ship and the SLT is the rudder, you only need one member of that team to pull to port or starboard at inconvenient times and the ship will deviate. We know that the shortest distance between two points is a straight line, and it is impossible to steer a straight course when you are continually correcting directional deviations.

"He who loves practice without theory is like the sailor who boards ship without a rudder and compass and never knows where he may cast."

Leonardo da Vinci

According to Miles Kierson, the word "Team" seldom belongs in the phrase Leadership Team. Miles describes Leadership Teams or Management Teams as a group of people who regularly get together for meetings and then return to their own departments and continue pursuing their own agendas. I can imagine many of you as you read this nodding your heads in agreement as I did when I read it for the first time. Most of us who have experienced SLTs firsthand recognize the situation, and we can all probably think of individuals who have let their oar trail in the water and deflect us off course, making the rest pull harder to correct the deviation and reach the finish line. If we are honest with ourselves, we may even admit that, at times, we have been the one with the oar trailing in the water, but human nature is such that we always prefer to see ourselves as one of the good guys.

Look at the title of this chapter closely and study the word "malignant." It is not a nice word, is it? It implies seriously bad things, and we associate serious health issues with the word. Alignment, however, is something that implies order and unity in purpose. The two words are at odds with each other.

However, if we simply move/relocate the letter "m" and then mess with the letter "a" by turning it on its head so that the "a" becomes an "e" and the word malignant is transformed into the word alignment. Sometimes small adjustments can create dramatic transformations.

malignant

alignment

To transform your leadership team from Malignant to Alignment, you just need to shift the "M and change the "A" you need to shift the **M**indset and change the **A**ttitude.

Everyone on the team needs to accept responsibility for achieving the team's objectives and do their utmost to achieve those objectives even if they do not agree 100% that they are the right objectives. Only when the mindset of those who do not fully agree with the objective is such that they accept that the team has chosen it and that now they must support it fully, only then can you say that you have an aligned team. To develop such a mindset in every team member develops confidence that the plan will move forward with the support of every member of the SLT and have a much better chance of success. All we need to do now is pay attention to the crew and make sure that the crew has the same attitude towards achieving our goals.

Hold on a second; this makes a lot of sense but is it thinking like da Vinci? We may be aligned but what exactly are we aligned behind? Should we be aligned with the organization's objectives? The shortest distance between two points is a straight line but does that make it the quickest route or the best route? What if that straight line has some EOS rocks submerged below the surface, waiting to scupper our plans and ruin our objectives? What if we meet with headwinds and the only way to make headway requires us to tack left and right? Would we want the one member of the crew who sees an iceberg to swerve us away from it or stick to the agreed course?

I think that we can all see that organizational alignment is a complex subject and that dedication to an objective is much less important than dedication to the well-being of the ship, its crew, and the passengers.

The Titanic sank not because the crew was in alignment; it sank because they were malignant. The owners were focused on setting records. They were more interested in the publicity and the marketing of those records to generate future business and profits than the single need of their collective customers to arrive safely at their destination. They overruled the captain and ordered him to increase speed; the crew was ill-prepared and unrehearsed for launching lifeboats. The designers felt that the boat was unsinkable, so they provided too few lifeboats, and some passengers were considered more important than others and were allowed to leave the ship quickly in half filled boats while the others were left to drown. The owners of the White Star Line put their own egos and their future profits before the needs of their customers and like the Titanic, their organization sank to the bottom and disappeared. You could say that in some ways, they were aligned behind the record-breaking objective, but clearly the malignancy set in by being aligned behind the short-term profit-driven needs of the organization and not the needs of the customer.

"He who wishes to be rich in a day will be hanged in a year."

Leonardo da Vinci

Alignment is essential but if we think like da Vinci, we will see that being aligned behind business-focused objectives is not the answer unless those objectives align with the needs of the customer. We need to be aligned with our passengers and our customers and ensure that we are seen by them to be doing everything we can to get them to their destinations and to meet their own objectives. The Titanic was as pure an example of a Malignant SLT as you will ever see. They failed miserably to meet their utmost objective, which was to get their customers, their passengers safely to their destination. When everyone in the organization aligns with the customer and pulls together to help customers achieve their objectives and meet their goals, they travel with you repeatedly. It is good to have someone put an oar in the water to avoid a collision it is smart to tack left and right to meet your customer's deadlines rather than to battle late delivery headwinds and avoid the hidden rocks. **Never confuse agility with inconsistency.** The ability to be agile and quickly respond to changes in the marketplace requires the organization to be aligned with the customer. The customer is the marketplace.

Does everyone need to be aligned and on board with this philosophy on day one? Ideally yes, but if you wait for that to happen, you might never leave the port. Remember from earlier, "To move forward, you must make a move." My personal philosophy is to try and get most of the team aligned and set sail. You can gradually get the rest of the crew facing the right way after you have set sail, you must avoid analysis paralysis.

I once implemented a Measurable Management® Program in a carpet manufacturing company in the UK. The Managing Director was full of enthusiasm for the program but some of the crew were less enthusiastic. His Training Manager was one of the "we already do this" brigade and his Manufacturing Director told his supervisors that his department was "a dictatorship and not a democracy."

The Managing Director could have made the mistake of staying in port until he got them all "on board" with the initiative, but he made a leadership decision to do what he thought would be best for his customers and best for his business and he launched the Measurable Management® initiative. Very quickly the manufacturing supervisors climbed on board and started making comments that those guys upstairs (primarily their own boss) needed to be doing this. The Training Manager, who was a course participant, started making changes to improve the quality of training and started walking the walk. The Manufacturing Director did not come on board at all until the voyage was over and he witnessed with his own eyes the improvements that his team had implemented. He gave them no support and I took the liberty of acting as a surrogate manager to encourage them to move forward. He sat in the presentation meetings, listening to the participants present one improvement after another and watched them bathe in the glory of their success as their actions were recognized and rewarded. It dawned on him at that point that he should have been more involved and less cynical and on the next voyage, he was precisely that.

Many leaders see the obvious benefits that a Measurable Management® approach can bring but make the mistake of putting it off because of other initiatives. Too many times I've heard the words, "We have too many other things going on right now and I don't want to burden them with something else, let's talk again in six months".

Hopefully, they will not hit any rocks in that six-month delay. Hopefully, they have enough lifeboats for all their customers if they do hit the rocks and they don't lose too many of them. The reality is that if these other initiatives are seen by those captains of industry as the lifeboats that will save their customers and hopefully, their organization, then Measurable Management® is a lifejacket for every passenger and every crew member. It does not displace existing initiatives, it sits within them and adds value and momentum. It gives everyone more confidence to step into the lifeboat. It gives those existing initiatives a real boost, like fitting a turbocharger to the engine.

Shifting the mindset begins at the helm, but it takes some bravery to make that customer-focused commitment. Can you really put the customer's needs before your own company's needs? The captain needs to align behind the customer first and then he or she must align the crew without delay. For the organization to become shipshape, a positive attitude towards the customer must be the utmost priority whether they serve the customer directly or work in the engine room. Getting the customer safely and efficiently to their destination matters much more than breaking records. Measurable Management® is designed to help you achieve this. It will provide the tools that are essential to align your organization behind your customers and bring order and efficiency to those existing lifeboat initiatives swiftly and effectively. If you think that you need to defer doing this because you have too much on your plate, then you do not understand that Measurable Management is not additional food on the plate—it is simply a bigger spoon.

CHAPTER TEN

WHERE'S YOUR BRIDGE?

We have all heard the old proverb "Too many cooks spoil the broth" and even the now politically incorrect "Too many Chiefs ...." The implication in these proverbs is that when too many people are involved in decision-making, their conflicting perceptions of the right solution will create chaos and a satisfactory solution will never be found. There is some truth to this view if you are talking about an organization that is not aligned with the satisfaction of the customer.

I asked the people at the carpet manufacturing company that I mentioned earlier to describe in one sentence precisely what it was that their company did. As we went around the table listening to their responses, you could be forgiven for believing initially that they were an aligned team because of the similarity in each response.

"We make the highest quality Wilton and Axminster carpets in the world," said one.

"We sell the best Wilton and Axminster carpets in the world," said another

"We design the finest Wilton and Axminster carpets in the world," said a third and so on.

The reality is that everyone looked at what their organization does from the perspective of their own department. The manufacturing department "makes the highest quality," the sales department "sells the best," and the design department "designs the finest Wilton and Axminster carpets in the world." Each was looking at their world through their eyes and looking at what the company did from their own department's perspective. If they had taken one step further and looked at their world through their customers' eyes, they would have written some different responses such as, "They make really expensive carpets." "Their designs are somewhat old fashioned," or "You need to order well in advance so as not to be kept waiting."

Many reading this will say, and it is true that "we already do that, we've already taken that step and we already look at our world through the eyes of the customer." This is good but why take only one step when you can take two? To be an organization that thinks like da Vinci you need to look at your customers' world through the eyes of the customer. Looking at your world through the eyes of the customer can fool you into feeling like you are customer-focused, but you are still focused on you and your products. Think of it this way, a cargo ship has the bridge towards the stern so that the crew can keep an eye on the cargo, the products. A passenger ship has a bridge towards the bow so that it can see ahead without obstruction and keep its passengers and crew safe. Are you looking after the cargo and your products, or are you taking care of your passengers, your customers and your crew?

To take care of your paying customers you need to move the bridge forward and allow team leaders and frontline managers who regularly interact with your customers the vision to make the swift and crucial decisions that will affect customer satisfaction.

If you are not agile your future is fragile. If you do not respond quickly to those changes in the marketplace and give the passengers what they want, they will find alternative transport.

Making the front line accountable, therefore, is not ending up with too many cooks; it is making the organization more agile. You only spoil the broth if you are putting in more salt when the customer is asking for pepper.

CHAPTER ELEVEN

DON'T SPIT IN THE SOUP

Imagine someone starting their own business making furniture perhaps. This person is a good carpenter and quickly finds themselves in demand. They cannot keep up with the demand, so they employ another carpenter to help. Soon, he or she realizes they need someone to handle the customers because they need to keep an eye on production. He or she is now one step away from the customer. They need to employ a bookkeeper to handle invoicing and accounts. If the customer has an invoice issue, they will talk to the salesperson, who speaks to the accounts person who gets the OK from the boss to issue a credit. He or she is now two steps away from the customer. It is quite easy to see that as organizations grow, it is extremely easy for senior managers to get further and further away from the customer and the further away the authority to act and respond to the customer, the more frustrated the customer becomes. This can be a problem for a medium-sized business, so imagine how far removed from the everyday customer the SLT of a Fortune Company can be. It is not enough to empower department heads you must empower the person who stands eye to eye with the customer. You must empower everyone.

When I first moved to the USA to live, I encountered something called the "mail-in rebate." For those outside the USA, this is basically a discount off the price, but in order to get your discount, you have to mail in your request for the rebate along with copies of the receipt, you must cut out and include the actual bar code from the packaging, provide any other proof of purchase and do all this within so many days from the date of purchase. If you bother to do all of this, then you should receive your rebate, which is usually in the form of a prepaid credit card. This assumes of course, that you have not received a letter saying that the rebate couldn't be processed because you sent a photocopy of the bar code and not the actual barcode cut from the box or they lost one of the documents and blame you for not sending it. They just spat in your soup.

The only reason that I can see for offering a mail-in rebate rather than just discounting the price at the cash register is that the company hopes that some will never apply for their rebate and that others will give up applying if they meet with an obstacle and that some will leave it until it is too late. In each of these cases the company ends up selling you their product at the full price and makes more profit than if they just gave everyone the discount.

Fred Reicheld, in his book, *The Ultimate Question,* refers to these kinds of profits as Bad Profits. These kinds of profits lower your Net Promoter Score by clearly frustrating the customer and destroying your chances of ever getting them to promote you and your products or services to anyone else. My decision was to refuse to buy anything that had a mail-in rebate. I did not want them spitting in my soup and if there are others like me, then the profits from those that buy are cancelled by the lost sales of those who walk away. Lost opportunities to satisfy a customer and have them tell others about their experience. This kind of promotion can easily create more detractors for you than it does for promoters. Thankfully, today it is a practice that appears to have died.

I once purchased a cell phone from a local store of a well-known American cellular network provider. As soon as I discovered it was being offered with a mail-in rebate, I told the store manager that, "I don't do mail-in rebates." He instantly offered to do the mail-in rebate for me at the store and gave me the cash discount on the spot. The agility of the organization to do this was created by moving the bridge to the front of the ship. Letting frontline managers make decisions that satisfy the customer. It is a good example but how much better if the initial conflict had been avoided altogether by kicking these Bad Profit tactics into touch. When marketing departments come up with promotions, they need to make sure that they please their customers and are not simply increasing the size of the sales prevention department. **Any person in the organization who fails to see themselves as part of the customer service team is part of the Sales Prevention Department.**

Sometimes we get things wrong, we make a mistake, and the customer expresses their dissatisfaction. Even a complaint is a great opportunity to show the customer that you really care and want to do the best that you can for them. If they send back the soup don't spit in it! Embrace a complaint as an opportunity to meet and exceed their expectations and guarantee a return visit.

Sadly, some people spit in the soup. I know that this is a disgusting analogy, but some organizations find it hard to accept that their wonderful products and outstanding service could ever fail to satisfy the customer and when they get a complaint, they blame the customer.

If you've ever tried to return a bad purchase and met with obstacles and resistance, then they just spat in your soup. Will you go back to that restaurant? I doubt it.

I know that Henry Ford once said, "If I asked my customers what they wanted, they would have said a faster horse."

We don't always know as customers what products or services will captivate us, so how do we as suppliers know what our customers don't?

I once read that to remain essential, you must think past what your customers know. You must solve the problems they've yet to encounter. Anticipate like a good fighter. This smacks of "thinking like da Vinci," but the danger here is that quotes like Henry Ford's can perpetuate the myth that innovation is somehow disconnected from customers, that you are smarter than them and you will fly in like Superman and save the day. Henry simply needed to ask the question, "Why do you need a faster horse?" By making the emotional connection to his customer it would have opened a dialogue that could have made it even easier to sell even more cars even faster.

If da Vinci was fully immersed in the Zone and Einstein paddled up to his knees, then by comparison, Henry just about got his toes wet. Getting your toes wet, however, is fantastic and is probably much closer than most others will ever achieve. Henry was reaching for the Zone.

Who on your management ladder is closest to the customer? Clearly it must be the person standing on the lowest rung. Your team leaders, supervisors, first-line managers, or whatever job title they hold according to the type of organization that they are working in. These front liners are the closest members of the leadership team to the customer.

When organizations talk about where to start, "should we take a top-down or bottom-up approach?" I often respond It doesn't matter where you start, just as long as you start. Measurable Management® targets everyone but perhaps you could start by focusing on the Team Leader, the first rung of the ladder. It's one step above the bottom and depending on how flat or otherwise the organization is, it's usually more than one step below the top. If you really believe that you need to move the bridge forward, then move it!

Your team leaders and first-line managers are the linchpins between your envisioned future and the people who will get you there. Their direct reports have their hands on the day-to-day processes that serve the customer. This is where the wealth of the organization is created, this is where the customers are ultimately engaged and are either satisfied or otherwise. If you are serious about wanting to engage the customer and are not just paying lip service, then team leaders and first-line managers are your lifelines. If you want to translate strategy into action, you need to develop this level of leadership as your number one priority and give them the opportunity to become accountable to the customer.

Measurable Management provides you with a simply packaged, customer-focused strategic and personal development program that targets everyone. To quote the

Southwestern Lean Summit organizers yet one more time,
"It is unnervingly simple yet powerfully effective."

"Simplicity is the ultimate sophistication."

Leonardo da Vinci

Chapter Twelve

Shackles or Anchors?

We have talked an awful lot so far about customer focus and taking care of the passengers aboard the ship. So, to keep our naval analogy going, let's talk about taking care of the crew.

Remember our reception area decorated with certificates that show our dedication to customer service, employee well-being and community conscience? Well, we need to balance the scales a little and look at employees and the community in more detail.

As the participants on the Measurable Management Program steadily evaluate their resources, relationships and processes, the program focuses them into some key learning points that they may want to pay extra attention to. As they review the many resources that they have at their disposal the program uses some very entertaining group exercises to demonstrate very graphically that our two most valuable resources are people and information. We can outperform our competitors, who may have much more up-to-date equipment and facilities, if our people are motivated and if we are better informed. If we can outperform the competition by ensuring our people are motivated imagine what we can do on the occasions that they are inspired.

In times long gone, the British Navy used Press Gangs to basically kidnap recruits from merchant ships and the bars of the local inns and force them into service. Some were even shackled when the ship was in port to prevent them from deserting.

It's probably a safe assumption that our employees today are volunteers and come to work each day of their own free will without the need for violent coercion, but we still use shackles to keep them onboard and prevent them from abandoning ship in favor of a life elsewhere. You may think that shackles are too strong a piece of imagery, but at what point does a health care plan, for example, stop being a benefit and become a shackle? I'm sure that in the USA, we've all heard people say things such as, "I'd work somewhere else, but I can't afford to lose my health plan." Another example might be, "I only need to stick it out for another four years and I'll get my pension." Such situations tell me that these individuals have been de-motivated and are unlikely to exceed performance expectations.

Don't misunderstand the message here, benefits are good, but bribery is bad. If coming to work is unsatisfying and if people feel uninvolved or unrecognized, then they come to work every day and very likely they will do an average job. If they could leave and know for sure that they would be secure from a health and financial perspective, then they would, in all probability, leave. This is the point that their benefits become the shackles that keep them on board and stop them from running. It's almost as if the corporate benefits are the bribe to keep them coming in every day to keep the corporate machine running.

Clearly, we will never be able to reach for The da Vinci Zone and do phenomenal things unless our crew is inspired. All we must do is repeatedly practice our listening and involving style—our Pull Style. When people feel that they are valued and their work has real meaning, the reasons to leave are dramatically reduced. When this happens the benefits stop being shackles and become much more like an anchor that provides stability but can be pulled up to allow progress to be made safe in the knowledge that the anchor is still there for when it's needed.

The benefits are secondary to the necessity of making the work interesting and satisfying. Making the work enjoyable has obvious impacts on productivity and the stability of the workforce. With the extra revenues that come from improved efficiency, increased productivity, reduced re-work and reduced attrition, it becomes more affordable to do things that make life even better for your employees by providing services for them that really add value to their working lives. Daycare for the children of employees, gymnasium facilities that keep workers fit and save them from expensive membership fees, good quality restaurant facilities on site, flexi-time work schedules, generous maternity leave for husbands as well as mothers, and extended vacation allowances.

I have long since believed that there is more productivity to be gained from a worker who takes five weeks of paid vacation than a worker who only takes two or three weeks of paid vacation. Remember that if it feels like pain, it's hard to sustain. Work that becomes routine will eventually become drudgery. We need finish lines and rewards. The last Friday night before vacation feels like crossing the finish line—the vacation is the reward.

What about those who don't respond to our positivity? I hear you ask. What about those who reap the rewards and still do an average job? What if we pulled and pulled and they didn't move or at least not as far as we had hoped they would move?

Then it's time to Push.

Most people and I really do mean the vast majority will respond well to a Pull Style of leadership, but when all else fails, give them a push. If they respond to the push, you need to see it and start pulling again. I had a poor-performing salesman working for me when I became

Commercial Sales Manager for Xerox in Leeds, England back in the eighties. I coached and counseled, I helped him get additional training, I enquired if everything was OK outside of work, and I went on field accompaniment with him to see how he performed in front of customers. No improvement! Time to Push!

I called him into my office and issued a formal warning for poor performance. Three formal warnings and you lose your job.

Now I know that at this point in the story, you want to hear that he improved and to be fair, he did improve a little for about a month, but two more formal warnings later, he was given the ultimate push, and I terminated his employment. It was regrettable but I did so in the knowledge that both myself and the company had extended every opportunity and incentive that we could think of before we decided that we had the wrong resource. We've all used a knife when we didn't have a screwdriver but ultimately, we go out and buy a screwdriver. Sometimes we must admit that the resource is not appropriate for the job, and we need to replace it. I met the same salesman sometime later and he thanked me for my help and then he thanked me for pushing him into the unemployment line. He recognized that selling was not going to be his vocation and he needed a career that made him feel more comfortable and less stressed out. He had since settled into a role in HR Management and appeared to be enjoying his new career.

It is never pleasant terminating someone's employment for performance reasons, and it is wrong to do so if you have not made every effort to help them help themselves. We must remember though that ultimately, we are trying to serve our customers as best we can. We are trying to get the paying passenger safely to their destination and to do that, we have to manage resources, manage relationships and control processes. If the unreliable resource is a person and they don't respond to our efforts and fail to meet the requirement, then we need to change the resource for one that does meet those requirements.

You wouldn't keep using the wrong tool if it damaged your materials or made you work twice as hard and reduced the quality of the finished outcome.

The salesman in my example couldn't improve as a salesperson because he didn't enjoy the role. He felt pain and there was no gain but was it his entire fault?

We may have to admit to ourselves that initially we are at fault. Why did things not work out with this employee? Was it a resource, a relationship or a process issue or a combination of these areas that gave us the undesired outcome? Maybe we need to look at our recruitment process? Maybe we need to look at our training providers?

Maybe we need to use experienced people to partner with new recruits? Maybe we missed an opportunity to strengthen our own HR team from within? The point I'm making here is that the failure to perform might have been a failure on our part just as much as it was a failure on the part of the salesman. Getting that right is the priority to reduce the risk and avoid incurring the costs of the same thing happening again.

Unlike the Press Gang techniques employed in days gone by, we can help to maintain a content workforce if we recruit well, train well and develop working relationships that motivate each other. Constructing these solid foundations allows us to build and grow in the knowledge that the organization cares about the people who work for it.

What about the community? You might agree that there is a huge business benefit to doing positive things for the employee, but doing things for the community sounds expensive.

> Joseph Rowntree 1836 – 1925 was a renowned philanthropist and businessman. I noted with interest that when I looked up his Wikipedia credits, they placed his philanthropy ahead of his huge success as a businessman. His company, Rowntree's of York in England, is a major chocolate

company in the UK and many people all over the world will have eaten one of their Kit Kat chocolate candies or one their many other branded products. They are today under the ownership of Nestle, though the Rowntree name and brand continue to be used.

Joseph Rowntree was a true champion of social reform and to quote Wikipedia, "Even as a powerful businessman, he was deeply interested in improving the quality of life of his employees; this led to him becoming a philanthropist, pursuing many charitable causes. While he was still living, he gave half of his money to the four Rowntree Trusts, which are dedicated to social reform and continue today."

I lived in York, England, from 1982 until 1986, and both of my daughters were born there. My next-door neighbor, Barry Plues, worked for Rowntree's. It would have been very hard for anyone to live in York and not know someone who worked for Rowntree's. Barry wasn't a manager, he was a worker and he made Kit Kats. He worked shifts, sometimes days, sometimes nights and he liked his job. I would go as far as saying that it was evident to anyone that from talking to Barry, he was proud to be a Rowntree worker. In 1936, my own father left home in County Durham at the young age of 17 and lived in lodgings at Mr. & Mrs. Deighton's home in New Earswick, York, some 80 miles from his parent's home to work for Rowntree's. He told me of how happy he was there and how he might have been there for many years had World War Two not come along and conscripted him into the British Army.

I find it interesting that my dad had consecutive jobs indirectly working for inspirational leaders, Joseph Rowntree and Winston Churchill. Admittedly, JR had died a few years earlier but his legacy lives on and still survives him to this day. The fact that Barry and my father spoke so highly of the firm is undoubtedly directly rooted in the vision of Joseph Rowntree.

J R aged 16

Joseph worked with his brother at his brother's cocoa
works and when his brother Isaac passed away in 1883, JR

took over the ownership of the small chocolate factory and, by the end of the 19th century, had grown his company from 30 to 4000 employees. He started one of the very first occupational pension schemes and set up what has become known as the Joseph Rowntree Foundation. If you look at their website, you will find that JR "wanted his money to be used to tackle the root causes of social problems, rather than treating their symptoms." He built homes for his workers in New Earswick, free schools for their children, he gave them a doctor, a social welfare officer, a library, and a dentist. His philanthropy developed and extended beyond his workers to the greater community of York and beyond.

If you want to learn more about the social and political impact that Joseph Rowntree had on British society, then feel free to investigate the web and elsewhere. I'm simply pointing out that many years ago, before today's modern philanthropists came to our attention, Joseph Rowntree was one of the first to recognize the value and downright goodness of doing positive things for your community.

Milton S Hershey, another famous chocolatier some 20 years younger than JR, used the exact same model to build an empire in the USA. Both were known for their philanthropy, and both lived into their late eighties.

Behaviour begets behaviour. Doing good and positive things for your community creates positive perceptions in the minds of that community and in turn positive attitudes that influence positive behaviors and good things for your organization.

Joseph Rowntree grew his company to 4000 employees in a dramatically short period of time. He grew it with goodness. He removed the shackles and became their anchor.

"Who sows virtue reaps honor."

Leonardo da Vinci

Chapter Thirteen

Turn On the Taps

That's pretty much it.

I hope that my perspective has piqued your interest even if I am often critical of traditional approaches to quality improvement, HR and Training and Development methods. These traditional approaches have merit but seriously lack efficiency in terms of getting things done and making things happen in a way or in a timeframe that restricts what is possible. In Measurable Management we took a significant leap forward in terms of providing individuals and organizations with a vehicle for getting important things done at high velocity, translating good intentions into positive outcomes. Even the US Air Force used similar words when they said that *"it is without doubt the most effect program that we have ever encountered for making things happen"*. The United Nations NGO Positive Peace Award committee referred to "its' phenomenal ability to deliver positive outcomes."

I learned very quickly that CEOs were very interested and extremely enthusiastic, about the idea of implementing my approach, and those with vision quickly saw the bigger picture and became excited about introducing a significant shift in culture. Unfortunately, with training departments and HR departments, the message often fell on deaf ears. Some, I think, saw it as a threat to their self-built empires and took the "Not invented here attitude" while others appeared a little nervous or unsure of breaking the mold by trying to do something that seemed radical to them. Only a very small percentage of training managers got excited by the idea and embraced it. I made it my intention, therefore, whenever possible, to only speak with senior leadership when meeting with organizations. When the HR Dept. would say things like "We don't have any money left in the training budget for it this year." They were either making an excuse or were simply unable to grasp that this wasn't about training budgets at all, it was about getting things done. Whatever the senior team needs to get done is where the money to fund the program is going to come from. It becomes financed as part of the budget allocated to those projects, objectives, key issues, or whatever it is that the organization needs to make happen.

I used to teach Measurable Management in the classroom to participants who were given a participant manual and attended group meetings every 2 to 4 weeks over a 6-month period. It took a large, licensed network of partners and frequent train-the-trainer sessions to provide the necessary numbers of facilitators to make all of this happen. Today we have created the online version that can be found at www.measurable-management.com (don't forget the hyphen). We have created an approach to suit all preferred learning methods with a true consistency of quality. I hope that you check it out.

If your existing initiatives are losing momentum, then add a supercharger to them. EOS or Traction is an initiative that can benefit enormously from Measurable Management. When EOS gives you 90 days or whatever to clear a rock that is preventing progress, Measurable Management is the stick of dynamite that EOS forgot to supply you with. You'll find that you won't need 90 days.

If you are serious about wanting to reach for The da Vinci Zone and if you wish to make giant leaps at high velocity, then why not try dipping your toes into the water? That's what the image on the front cover of this book is all about. Open all the stop valves and unleash the hidden talent. Flood your workplace with creativity, inventiveness and artistry. As we have already stated more than once, the best consultants that you could have, already work for you. Give them permission to reach, give them permission to make the odd mistake, give them recognition for their successes, and prepare to be amazed at how quickly they make change happen.

Go ahead! Transcend your perceived limitations and don't let your doubts or the doubts of others talk you out of it. Reach for The da Vinci Zone and remember:

"If you want to do unreal things, it is absolutely OK to be unrealistic."

Robin Byrne

ABOUT THE AUTHOR

Robin Byrne has dual citizenship as both a British and US citizen. He ran operations for Xerox UK in the Northeast of England before setting up his own company in 1992 to help businesses get things done and make things happen. He authored the Measurable Management Program and in 2011 this was nominated for the United Nations NGO Positive Peace Award for delivering "phenomenal outcomes into nonprofit organizations". He's a member of Equity, the actor's union, and also directs theatrical productions.

Website: www.measurable-management.com